Best of Trail's End
BY JIM DOUGHERTY

Volume 1

Brought to you by the Editors of

Best Of Trail's End

Credits

Editor: Jay Michael Strangis
Production Coordinator: Carolyn Olson
Associate Editors: Daniel Beraldo, Ryan Hamre
Art Director: Nicole Mahany
Prepress: ArrowTrade Publishing
Publisher: Petersen's Bowhunting

First Edition

Library of Congress Cataloging-in-Publication Data
ISBN: 1-892947-77-3

Contents

Chapter 5   Strange Happenings

Chapter 6   Other Critters

Chapter 7   Mailbag

Chapter 8   Exceptional Animals

Chapter 9   Friends & Family

Chapter 10   Deer with White Tails

INTRODUCTION

It's been a long, long time, 20 years I'm thinking, maybe more since Greg Tinsley, *Petersen's Bowhunting's* first established editor called one evening and asked if I would be interested in writing Trail's End for the magazine. Honestly, I was both surprised and flattered, back pages are pretty good duty!

Well, that was as I said a long, long time ago, so much so that I cannot honestly recall what year it was or what I wrote about. *Petersen's* was a fairly new magazine with just six issues a year, not nearly as many pages and nowhere near the depth of writing talent we have now, or the reputation for being a mainstream periodical.

I lay becoming a mainstream magazine at the feet of Jay Strangis. Tinsley moved on to other things (rumor has it he's fly fishing in West Point, Mississippi) and Jay became our new editor with a bunch of timely notions on how to make things happen. I figured when I heard the news I was a "goner" though Jay soon called, eased my fears, gave me a raise and told me to continue doing what I was doing. And so I have... whatever I'm doing seemed good enough.

Trail's End is mostly ramblings based on my 50 some years of bowhunting experiences. It brings friends, adventures and places together designed, I hope, to entertain. For the most part it offers no advice on how-to, though it is not without the occasional firm opinion on a subject I hold near and dear. These opinions you may take as gospel!

As writing books goes, this is the way to do it. You crank out columns and forget them as you approach the next, working I might add several months in advance, which screws with your mind when it's February but the next issue is May/June. Then, one day someone calls and says they're going to make a book out of some of your columns. That's cool! There is really nothing to do, it's already done. Not at all like a book I've been working on for three years starting from scratch that still has a long ways to go.

I find it strange and lucky that I've gotten to this point, I have no training in writing, no journalistic background, heck, I barely passed high school English, but I have a lifetime of training in archery from way back when I was a little kid stalking birds in the yard. I met Doug Kittredge when I was 13 when he was just opening his famous Bow Hut. I asked for and received a job, and thus my career in the archery industry began. In 1957 after winning the Worlds Championship Varmint Calling Contest down in Arizona, Roy Hoff, the Editor and Publisher of *Archery Magazine* asked me to write something about calling for him. I did, and as they say, the rest is history.

So there you are, a brief capsule of how this whole thing got started. Trail's End is more than a column to me, it's a place where I can go to reflect on things past, to contemplate the future, to even rant on occasions when it seems necessary to me. I hope you will enjoy my efforts.

Jim Dougherty

DEDICATION

This is for Sue, who has put up with all of my hunting stuff since she was sixteen. She is a wonderful wife and mother, a helluva cook and my very best friend.

Chapter 1

Early Lessons

Shooting
Before
The Wheel

My first real bow, the one I progressed to after backyard sticks and a store-bought York lemon wood 25-
pounder, was really sort of a club.

I grew up in Southern California. The shooting ranges of
the Pasadena Roving Archers, Sagittarius (the nation's first
broadhead club) and the Pasadena Target Archers were all laid
out in tandem along the lovely, live-oak shaded bottom of
Lower Arroyo Seco Creek. When I was a kid, I fished for wild
rainbow trout in the creek, a semi-wild place just close enough
from home to reach on my bicycle.

Sometimes when I trekked to the creek, there would be an
archery tournament. In fact, I was there during the 1949
NFAA Championships. You couldn't fish or explore when a
tournament was being held, so I watched. I never got over it.
When the archers settled in at full draw, you could honestly
feel the intense vibration of stretched bowstrings, followed by
a world of whistling shafts. Somehow, every time, they all let
go at once. I wondered, even after I started doing it, how that
worked. It was great fun for a kid to watch. I saw it as a reen-

actment of medieval firepower–the first artillery in its original form.

An old man gave me my first bow. He had a half-dozen lemon wood, yew, and hickory longbows in his truck. I guess he made them himself; I never found out. I only saw him once more after that, when they caught me sitting behind the target butts during a tournament. I wanted to know what the arrows sounded like before they hit the oil cloth. The officials were understandably annoyed at my interest. The old man was nice about it. After the hysteria died down, he told me it was a stupid place to be. "You know, these things can kill you!" he said. That had never occurred to me.

The bow he had given me was 66 inches long. I know that because later Doug Kittridge built me a string, gaily wrapped in multicolored silk rod winding thread above and below the hand grip. I have wished a hundred thousand times I still had it. I don't even know what I did with it after a newer bow came along.

I started this out by saying the bow was a club. That's unfair. It was simply a bow that didn't fit me. "Fit" in those days meant whether or not you could handle the draw weight. In its day, it would have been considered a fair example of the bowyer's craft; "bowyers" being those folks who made them from scratch. Anyhow, it was simply too much draw weight requiring pure brute strength to pull any distance before letting loose. That's all I could do. Accuracy was not a consideration. I just wanted to see how far I could make the arrows go. They went pretty far; clear up the street to the Finnert's roof—point first—probably 150 yards. I then decided that before I got caught, it was best not to shoot it in the neighborhood anymore.

Obviously hooked on this bow-and-arrow stuff, I was fortunate to wander into friendships that helped me become better equipped. I got involved in the entire scheme, though I realized even then when I was trying to shoot field and target rounds, something I was never too good at, that bowhunting was where the action was. I shot a lot of tournaments. We didn't know how fast our bows were then, we just drew back and let 'em rip. No matter how good you were, everyone had to hold somewhere on the top of the bale on the 80-yard walk up to drop one in the five ring. Trajectory we understood. Speed (we called it "cast") wasn't the issue, as true bowshooting skill was the dividing line. Buckskin shirts were popular along with heavy lace-up arm guards. A big shoulder quiver the size of a small wastebasket stuffed with arrows was a sign that you were with it. The well-heeled guys had tooled leather jobs. We sounded like junk wagons when we walked. A lot of archers wore those funky pointed hats with pheasant tail feathers, the kind Erroll Flynn wore in "Robin Hood". If you won something, like a 20-pin or a tournament medal, it was punched into a quiver shoulder strap or the rim of the funky hat. I had one of those hats.

Bows were evolving quickly. The competitive range has always been the point of conception for ideas and theory. Ink marks on the face side of risers gave way to real bowsights in real sight windows. Aluminum began to replace wood arrows. Harry Drake gave us really short bows that were under 60 inches. We called them "brush bows" as if you could go in to the brush and shoot them. Fiberglass technology was making things like that happen. Glass and wood composite recurves were in—longer ones for competition, short ones for the brush. You could tell what a guy was thinking by the bow he carried. Bowhunting seasons were different then, too. They were much shorter, if we had one at all. I spent a lot of my growing-up years at public hearings arguing for the right to bowhunt. That hasn't changed. Now we fight to keep what we have. Altogether, I spent more time trying to shoot cottontails, ground squirrels and jackrabbits than I ever did practicing for a tournament. I only won a few tournaments, but I shot a lot of rabbits. An NFAA Art Young Small Game Award was much more important.

I shot my first deer on a right-to-left running shot. It was pretty close, but still a great accomplishment. I had a 45-pound recurve, 62 inches long, and cedar arrows with real, barred turkey feathers, behind a Hills Hornet three-bladed broadhead filed to what I would consider today an inadequate edge. The arrow passed through the deer and buried up to the back of the head in an orange tree. The event took place in the orange grove where the tree lived, which was downtown Pasadena almost 40 years ago. I was 16 and thought I was Howard Hill. In 1961 and 1962 I shot 31 big-game animals, including my first antelope and bear, with a matched pair of 49-pound Howard Gamemasters. All were taken at close, hands-and-knees range with complete penetration. Today, some people shooting 80-pound compounds may find that incredible.

An archery shop in the '50s and '60s was a scented blend of aromatic Port Oxford cedar, crisp lacquers, comfortable real leather, and the occasional overpowering crush of burning feathers.

Some people hate the way things have changed. "Traditionalist" is sort of a buzz word for folks who like old styles, though they seem to ignore that computer-designed recurves with hi-tech glass aren't really traditional. Primitive longbow aficionados aside, recurve and longbows today are a far cry from what they were 40 years ago. It shouldn't matter. What does is that we all love the flight of an arrow, the challenge of putting it in the right place, and the company of people who share the feeling.

I never knew or properly thanked the man who gave me my first real bow. Kids are like that. I've given a lot of them away myself, and I'm sure as I get closer to being an old guy, I'll give away some more. He would have liked that.   ⟰

Early Lessons

I remember my first bowhunt for deer as clearly as if it happened yesterday. It took place 40 years ago this past July in Southern California's hot, rugged country—dusty-dry country with as many temperamental rattlesnakes as legal deer. Legal deer were "bucks only" with at least a forked antler on one side. It was a rather steep challenge given my experience (zero), equipment (rather primitive) and a rather scanty deer population.

My equipment consisted of a laminated semi-recurve bow of 45 pounds. It was a pretty modern weapon for those days, considering some of my friends were still packing around self-made bows of yew and lemon wood. At reasonable ranges—say, up to around 30 yards—we were pretty accurate, though I am sure none of us had any idea how "fast" our bows shot. If I had to make an educated guess, I'd say somewhere around 150 feet per second.

Imagine that!

This was in the days before bow quivers. We carried our

arrows in shoulder quivers like Howard Hill and Errol Flynn—it was the style of the times. We were modern-day Robin Hoods with brilliantly custom-crested shafts fletched with stout gray-barred turkey feathers dancing behind our string-hand shoulders. Our cedar shafts clattered in their leather housings; this was okay on the practice range, but for the serious business of hunting, we filled the bottoms with oatmeal to reduce the clatter and to protect our carefully honed hunting heads—Hill's Hornets, Bod-Kins, Hillbres and Ace Expresses.

My choice at the time was the Hill's Hornet, a three-blade without any connection to Howard Hill, though many folks thought so at the time. I sharpened the heads in a vise, carefully draw-filing them like Hugh Rich had patiently taught me. They were not as sharp as the modern insert-style heads of today, though eventually they would prove to be sharp enough time and again.

The oatmeal trick was Doug Kittredge's idea. He said if you got real hungry you could always eat it.

We always carried some blunts for small game, ground squirrels or rabbits. While the thought of getting a deer burned with a fierce fire, my quiver was already heavily decorated with NFAA Art Young Small Game pins and patches. We did that then, attaching the symbols of assorted triumphs to our quivers.

At daylight, everyone took off from the camp we had set in the dark the night before, scattering to various points of the compass. No plan, just go. In the cool of a morning that would soon melt into a 100-degree day, I angled downhill to one of those pretty Southern California wild trout streams that are now mostly nothing but silted in memories. Going toward water made sense to me.

At the head of a small draw studded with *manzanita*, I came across some deer tracks on the powdery ground of summer. I had no idea if they were buck or doe tracks, but, hey, I was deer hunting. Following those tracks made good sense to me in my youthful optimism, even though logic told me the odds were 50-50. So I tracked, easing along as quietly as possible, my very first big game still-hunting experience.

It seems I was blessed with a natural ability to move quietly; stalking cottontails, brush rabbits and long-eared jacks certainly helped refine my early technique even though I always seemed to make too much noise. Natural noise, though, as I learned over and over again in the years that followed, won't hurt you. I eased along slowly, looking carefully around and through each emerald green clump of red-stalked manzanita, just as I did when slip-hunting for cottontails. I peeked around another clump and swallowed fast just to keep my heart from jumping out of my throat. My entire body was jolted with the biggest adrenaline rush of my life. Twenty yards away was the twitching tail of a mule deer head-down facing dead away. I had never been this close to a live deer in my life!

I remember nocking the arrow that was in my hand while slowly sinking to my knees—I was finding it terribly difficult to stand. My legs were trembling with a run-amuck jiggling current that coursed through my body to the very tips of trembling fingers clutching my arrow to the string. The index finger of my bow hand tightened on the pulsating shaft, keeping it from going off somewhere by itself. I didn't even know what kind of deer I was looking at.

Then she raised up and broke the trembling, anxious spell, her smooth, illegal head letting me off the hook. She was surprised but not startled, cautious with her head-bouncing investigation of the trembling form hunkered in the brush. Finally, her foot-stomping head-bob was punctuated by an explosive snort that triggered her pogo-stick flight down the hill. While I watched her bounce away, a word picture of mule deer formed in my head: Boing! Boing! Boing!

Nobody got a deer on that hunt. Nobody honestly saw a buck, though someone—Doug Kittredge, I think—thought he might have seen one. It was late in the evening, and he just wasn't sure. Besides, the deer was a long way away, so it really didn't matter. What really mattered at that point in our lives was just doing it. We had a lot to learn, and school was just getting started.

A few frustrating seasons passed before success finally came my way. By then there had been several good opportunities, hard earned chances blown, easy shots missed for a hundred different reasons. Somewhere along the way, I passed the point of being intimidated. Sure, I still got excited (still do), but I guess what happened is I got tired of them beating up on me. I got mad at the deer and madder at myself. It worked out about the same for my hunting buddies, too, and things started to sort themselves out pretty well after that.

In the 40 years since that day, there have been a few successful stalks and no small number of major adrenaline surges, but never one quite like the very first. She was a nice ol' doe. I can still see her churning down that hill. Boing! Boing! Boing!

You know, I really owe her a lot.   ⚰

The First Bowhunt

Invariably when I visit with a crowd of archery hunters, the question arises, *When and how did you get started in bowhunting?* It seems so long ago now that explaining it should almost begin: *Once upon a time...*

Once upon a time, in Southern California, the Devil's Gate Dam kept the waters of Arroyo Seco Creek—a lovely, bubbling, then native wild trout stream—from seeping into the city of Pasadena, primarily the Rose Bowl grounds and the verdant golf links of adjacent Brookside Park. On the downstream side of the dam was an ugly concrete channel Southern California engineers seemed so fond of.

In the fall when the waterfowl migrated along the Pacific Flyway, the shallow lake and mud flats behind the dam held oodles of ducks, mostly pintails and green-winged teal. A smattering of almost every species of western waterfowl imaginable was also there. The broad valley behind the dam was a wild, natural place, with access not severely restricted. Fishing was allowed, but discharging firearms was a no-no.

At that time in my life—a high school junior—I was a bird hunter and angler. My father was an ardent waterfowler, and hunting for ducks and geese was our primary passion. Like most kids, I had a bow—a store-bought York lemonwood with a genuine leather-wrapped grip Dad had gotten for me—and a handful of really nice cedar arrows, which, for thousands of times, I've wished I still had just one.

Anyway, the wheeling, whistling flocks of sleek, long-tailed ducks close at hand were gnawing away at me. My lemonwood York sat close to my treasured Remington Model 11 on the rack in my room, with the quiver of sleek cedars alongside. It's not hard, if you're keeping up, to figure out the thoughts scurrying through my adolescent brain. While the discharge of high-brass sixes was plainly prohibited on the Devil's Gate marsh, there was nary a negative word about bows and arrows.

Realizing the necessity of preparation, I embarked on a serious tune-up involving a pair of our best full-bodied Victor decoys. In those days most decoys were made of treated papier-mache. Pounding them with steel-tipped arrows might have been realistic practice, but, as my father pointed out upon viewing the carnage, it wasn't a practical way to treat such valuable tools.

I didn't really feel as bad as I let on. The decoy practice did, however, build my confidence about shooting ducks. In fact, I dreamed that my duck strap would be burdened with a full limit, which, in those days, was 10! Bowhunting, I would come to learn, is a pastime filled with optimistic dreaming.

In my planning I had drawn in an accomplice, an older schoolmate named Stewart who shared my interest in waterfowl. As I had been smitten by his luscious sister at the time (not all of my thoughts were preoccupied by outdoor things), it seemed the politically correct thing to do.

Thus, on a certain Saturday in November we hunkered in the weeds and mud of the mucky shore as grey turned to silver on the eastern horizon. The air was filled with the whisper and flutter of wings tuned to the whistle of pintails, the strident peep of green wings. Soon the silver etched with wavering, lacy black lines. Distant dots ballooned into cup-winged birds at point blank range.

When it was light enough we picked a settled bird within range. We missed. We missed again and again in the early light as birds rose and settled. They flared away to circle and fall in concerned, perhaps, though certainly not panicked, by our silent barrage.

Our arrow supply was exhausted too quickly. Our precious shafts now floated among the ducks who while settling contentedly unmolested, swam and preened, quacked and gabbled as our ammunition drifted around them. Things didn't work out quite according to plan. Or did they?

In the years that followed I became a bowhunting fanatic. Within a few months of the *Great Duck Hunt*, fate threw me in the path of Doug Kittredge who opened his famous Bow Hut within walking distance of my home. We became lifelong friends, and I began my career in the archery industry running a spine meter, making bowstrings, cresting arrows and sweeping the Bow Hut's floors.

I never made another pass at the Devil's Gate ducks. Stewart's sister threw me over for a burly senior fullback, and we all went our separate ways. Doug introduced me to proper bows and arrows and how to use them. Bigger game than ducks began to fill my restless, ambitious dreams. Time passed with many lessons learned in the game fields of the world, though one lesson always remained constant and true: Things don't always work out as you had planned. Bowhunting's basic lesson was handed to me by a bunch of pintails.

It makes for a good reply though, when I'm asked about the beginning, how I got started bowhunting.

"Well son, I started out hunt'n ducks."

It gets their attention.

Verdugo Hills Mulies

We called it "Flat Spot". It was a bench that flattened and spread out for 50 yards along the steep, narrow-spined ridge that ran downhill due west and petered out in residential backyards of citizens of Burbank, California. The ridge that formed Flat Spot was a spur off the main north/south hump of the major peak on the west side of the Verdugo Hills. Flat Spot was about a half-acre in the shape of a football. The trail along the narrow spine that dropped to it was gouged and powdered by the passage of generations of slender mule deer hooves, and it was only wide enough for humans to travel single file.

In the early morning, if you happened to be sitting on the main ridge above Flat Spot, you could watch and listen as the San Fernando Valley cranked up and coughed to life. From my favorite vantage point, if the winds were calm, I could hear the tower at the Burbank Airport directing traffic. Listening to a throbbing city kicking in for another day, though, was not the reason for being there. The rugged terrain of the Verdugos—

like all the remaining small ranges of wilderness surrounded and dying under the tentacles of suburbia—hosted healthy numbers of Pacific Coast mule deer. These are smallish deer, no more than three-quarters of the size of the larger Rocky Mountain strain.

There were key spots in this sprawl of brush-covered hills with private names we all recognized and understood when campaign plans were formed in the early mornings at the Winchell's Doughnut spot in Glendale. We schemed in the dark hours before dawn over hot coffee and fresh dunkers: The places had names like The Blind Canyon, Round Top, George's Blind, Hills 101 and 102 and Flat Spot to give you some idea. We numbered around 10; some still bowhunt, nearly grizzled veterans now, while others have dropped away, their whereabouts and pastimes unknown. But, then, for all of us, charging the hills in hope of claiming a deer was life's main focus, and the plans we laid were, by experience, designed to accomplish that goal.

This is not easy country. Though main fire-control roads and breaks provided some access and rather easy going, in most cases, the best avenues to deer country began at the bottoms of treacherous, brush-covered ridges. Who would go where was decided. And who would come out where at noontime pickup points was determined.

Each individual hunt was crafted into a loose form of teamwork. In a sense they were drives over a widespread expanse. Years of doing it had given us clues to a pattern of routes. But it was not all ambush. Experience had taught us where to move and how fast, which little draws to peek into that the deer seemed to prefer, what stand of oak to sneak up on, what trails they might be working up along. Such knowledge oftentimes resulted in a clean, close-range shot.

We were armed differently than most of today's archery hunters. Recurves and compounds like we have today were unheard of; unimaginable. Lord knows, I never envisioned such a transition. We carried Howard Gamemasters, Citations by Tom Jennings, Red Wing Hunters, Bear Kodiak Specials and Magnums, Ben Pearson Mustangs. Our arrows were mostly silver-hued Easton aluminums; anodized shades of green and orange were someplace over the horizon. Some carried Micro-Flite glass shafts, others custom-crafted, high-quality cedar, all feather fletched.

We carried them in Bear Snap-On 8 Arrow Bow Quivers, or Silent Stalkers, a hip quiver that also held eight. It was not uncommon for someone to stumble wearily off the mountain completely out of arrows and in good humor. Our broadheads were mostly Zwickeys, Bear Razorheads, and Ace Expresses carefully filed and stoned to the best possible edge. We experimented in gluing razor blades to Bodins and liked the results. The first insert-style head we ever saw was the Little Shaver by the W.R. Brooks Co. It took full-length Schick injector blades. They were awesome, but not very tough if you missed and drove one into the rocky hillsides rather than a rib cage.

It was always hot, dry and dusty in the Verdugos. We carried canteens and snakebite kits. Sulky, black Pacific Coast rattlesnakes with angry buzzers were commonplace. We learned to watch the ground with one eye and deer with the other, an ingrained habit I maintain to this day. Though frequently startled, sometimes terrified, no one I knew of was ever bitten. Rattlers never bothered me mentally; it seemed I always saw them in time, except once when one miscalculated its strike and hung up in the loose drape of my camo pants just above ankle high!

On days when Flat Spot was on my itinerary, I could usually watch it long enough as the morning progressed to know what was there. Sometimes there was no indication, but, I was always willing to bet the comfortable place with its shaded bedding cover would have somebody at home. Win or lose on the flat, I would drop off the rest of the way, hit the canyon bottom and walk out to the residential road cul-de-sac where the nice lady with the very big house lived. We liked her. She wished we'd shoot every flower-eat'n deer on the mountain and was quite firm in her position.

If my memory's working right, I took seven deer off Flat

Spot over the years. I know George Wright took several, too. I wish I could be sure, but my field notes covering those 15 years or so are lost, probably in the transition to Oklahoma. I wish I had the notes, for those were the best bowhunting times. The exciting, learning times when rough hills were no intimidation to leaner bodies and tougher legs. Flat Spot is still there. If you know where to look you can see it off of Interstate 5, but, new housing will claim it soon. The nice lady's house is now so far into town there probably hasn't been a deer track in her flowers for years. I flew over it not long ago, going into Burbank. It made me kind of sad. And I thought about someone piddling in a new flower garden on the high-dollar terraced real estate and finding part of an old hunting arrow. I wonder if the arrow will tell them about the good times. ⬆

Chapter 2

Far Flung Places

Memories Of Mozambique

At Covane, the bare suggestion of a road broke away from the sandy delta of the Rio Save and climbed toward Repembe Camp. Out of the riverbed, the dim, rutted path coursed across an immense spread of arid country where it finally became lost in an area where the flies were especially bad. Rui said it was due to the vast herds of wandering wildebeest. He drove faster to avoid the stifling clouds of insects.

The highland crossing took us through stands of golden game-rich scrub bush and across crinkly, yellowing grassland prairie studded with the occasional baobab trees that punctured the horizon. Rui Quadros, my professional hunter, used them as landmarks to Repembe Camp, along with questioning glances to Sam or July, his trusted trackers/gunbearers, who gestured casually to keep him on course.

Repembe Camp sat in a small clearing adjacent to a dry riverbed of the same name. We went there because the map indicated it was an area of numerous small lakes. Water, especially in Africa, is the best hole card you can hold.

Licenses were generous then. The cost of a safari included most of the common game. I was allowed two impala, two wart hogs, two bush pigs, one reedbuck, one bushbuck, several of the various duikers, an oribi, two waterbucks and one buffalo. The first elephant was $125 and a second cost $265. I was allowed a second buffalo for $36. Most of the special critters had modest price tags. A sable antelope ticket was $43, a nyala was $72 and a greater kudu cost $43. Lions and leopards were 54 scoots U.S. There were several others, but you get the idea. Preparation of the trophies—skinned, cleaned and dipped for shipping—averaged five dollars apiece. I had booked a month for $3,200.

Safarilandia's quality concession in Mozambique was huge, nearly 8,000 square miles. Like other safari companies you may have heard about, hunting concerns in old Tanganyika, Kenya or Rhodesia had substantial blocks of granted land. The nice thing about Safarilandia was its experience with archery hunters.

Fred Bear and Dick Mauch had introduced me to Rui in the mid-1960's. We became good friends several years before my African dreams began to jell.

Rui Quadros was one of those rare men that you instantly liked, envied and resented just a little bit, all at the same time. He was one of those special guys that simply had it all together: He was multi-lingual, not counting African dialects, tanned and curly-haired, with a medium, wiry frame that suggested agile competence and power. He was the finest shot with a rifle or shotgun I have ever met, and I've met some very, very good ones. He showed up on my front porch in the spring of 1969 with a gold-trimmed leopard claw necklace, handed it to my wife and said, "Hullo, I'm Rui. This is for you. I came to meet you and to talk to Jim about going to Africa with me."

I'm not sure which of us wanted to go with him more.

At Repembe, the primary quarry was nyala. I managed a very good waterbuck, two wart hog, an oribi and a duiker. I missed many impala, shot quite a few guinea and fowl, but I never had a chance at a nyala. From Repembe, we headed for

Nhabende where kudu and bushbuck were the prime tickets. We saw a pile of nyala, one of which stood still too long; a bush pig; another duiker, the grey type this time; and I missed several more impala. No kudu. This was spot-and-stalk stuff. Hunting laws in the area forbade the taking of game within one-half mile of a water hole. We could shoot darting doves or whirring flocks of sand grouse in the technicolor evenings around water, but no big game. It struck me as a contradiction.

We kicked around in the Nhabende country for almost a week. It was prime kudu stuff. We finally made contact with the King of all Kudus; he was all by himself and seemed rather lazy and stupid. However, I missed him. Rui said he was easily 60-plus inches. The very next day we saw the Prince of all Kudus. This one was probably just 60 inches. I missed him, too. Late that afternoon, I shot a perfect arrow through a fine impala at a rather significant distance. Rui hardly acknowledged the event. The King of the Kudus weighed heavily on his mind.

I had no strong desire to shoot an elephant, though Rui wanted me to. I thought about that as we delayed our trip to Alves de Lima to track elephants. I was fairly certain I could kill one, but the question was, why? A medium bull, the size of a small condominium with tusks of maybe 30 pounds was the best we could locate. Rui was excited, I wasn't. I thought it would be very interesting to stand flat-footed and shoot a charging elephant—a good elephant—head-on with the proper rifle. I thought I could do that, but that's as far as my interest in elephant hunting went. I preferred to shoot kudu.

I got a kudu at Alves de Lima. He was hardly one of the Kings or Princes of Kududom, but he was a nice bull with 50-something horns—no monster—and certainly not the type of kudu we saw gracing the pages of the sporting journals. However, that didn't bother me then, and it doesn't bother me now. He's all mine, along with the memory of a perfect day that began with a good bushbuck, a neat little spiral-horned kudu cousin, another impala at noon and the kudu in the crimson glow of late afternoon.

I also remember the stand of yellow-fever trees we sat in when July hissed. Sam's eyes followed his, then met Rui's with a nod. I saw him then. Kudu always looked purple to me and there in the low-slung afternoon light he was a brilliant purple illuminated in a golden halo. Maybe it made him look bigger with his head cast back and the spiral of his horns shimmering, the white body stripes and nose chevron glowing. It didn't matter if he was extra big—I wanted him. He was everything that had drawn me to Africa.

This all took place nearly half a lifetime ago. It has been said that I was the last bowhunter in Mozambique, actually one of the very last hunters of any kind until just recently, when a few adventurers tested the hunting and political waters. Many of the fine people I met then are no longer alive, victims of a horrible, nasty revolution. Their land and homes are gone, the families scattered to the winds. Rui was run out, though he slipped back and forth to fight vigorously for what he felt was his. No one knows where he is today. I heard the revolutionaries shot July and most of the staff at the camp on the Rio Save at Zinave, but you never know for certain which stories are true.

If hunting Africa does anything especially well, it's to paint a picture for the scrapbook of your mind. I think though, before that happens, I have a date with another kudu. However, it will not be in Mozambique, and therefore it cannot be quite the same.

Rui won't be there, nor Sam or July with their keen eyes. Or will they? Somehow, I think they will.   ▲

Sunsets
And
Firelights

L ate in the evening, after the sunset slipped from gold-
en pink-streaked purple to deep, satiny black, the big
fire kept us awake. Campfires have a way of doing that.
African campfires hold you longer, though, probably because
you know there will never be quite enough of them.

We usually left camp very early, so the days were long and
full—the kind of days dreamed about and hoped for, the reason
you came. Sometimes we drove through swirling tendrils of
wispy pre-dawn ground fog hanging like smoke from a lost fire
across the open plains. I referred to them as "prairie", but Rui
called anything outside of camp "bush". The mornings were
crisp: A sweater or a light jacket were barely enough as the
open car purred through the gloom to some far-off spot Rui
and his trackers had selected. We hunted into late afternoon,
looking for that one good chance among a hundred maybes,
for the right critter in the right place for a stalk. Sometimes it
went well, sometimes not quite, but that was okay. It was
always exciting, the way bowhunting is supposed to be.

No matter how early we left, we always tried to make it back to camp in time for the sunset. It wasn't a requirement; no rule said we had to be there, and of course, there were times when we weren't. But somehow, most of the time, we were in camp for the sunset.

African sunsets are singular events. They are marvelously enjoyable from any perspective, though I came to believe they were best viewed and appreciated from camp. I suspect, after years of reflection, that those who cater to visiting hunters know this, and that is why they try to make it back to camp in time.

A few times, when we were heavily involved in a particular quest, we missed the sunset. Absorbed in the task at hand, the day ran out. Then an ink-black canopy fell over us—an eerie shroud in such a faraway, vast and rather scary place. The drives in the dark through a completely trackless wilderness were, to me, both mysterious and anxious. I could never figure out how we got ourselves back to camp.

When we arrived, sometimes quite late, everything was ready—as if someone had called ahead to say we were running a bit late. The tender broiled dove appetizers were always finger-licking hot. The wispy breeze bore the scent of a roasting impala, and the guy with the ice for your drink was always close at hand. At the edge of camp, in the glow of the fire and lanterns, the skinning crew tended to the cause of our tardiness. The breeze carried their soft-spoken conversation along with the whisper of steel and whetstone, mixed with the scent of roasting game. After dinner and showers, we sat by the big fire for a few extra minutes, the conversation fading to silence. Sometimes it's all right to miss a sunset.

Africa seems to be much on the minds of archery hunters today, more so, it seems, than Alaska or British Columbia. When I was a kid, those were the places we talked and dreamed about, places with moose, caribou, mountain goats and bears. We didn't talk about Africa—we hardly even thought about it, maybe because it was so far away.

Oh sure, some bowhunters had tackled Africa. There was Bill Negley, who went on a bet that he couldn't take an elephant with a bow, who said he couldn't lose. That certainly elevated the perception of a bow's effectiveness in those days. Of course, Fred Bear went. We all followed his adventures—he was our hero. His successes didn't hurt the perception of bowhunting either. Bob Swineheart went and took on the Big Five, and what most folks have forgotten is that Art Young and Saxton Pope had waded those perilous waters many years earlier. I guess it was because of Fred, though, that some of us started to think about Africa.

Of course, we talked about Fred during the sunsets—I suspect all bowhunters around campfires eventually do. Rui, my professional hunter, knew him. Wally Johnson, the senior professional hunter in the outfit, had guided Fred. Fred had been there, in some of the very same camps, watching the same sunsets. It seemed right to talk about him.

Today, a lot of archery hunters are taking on Africa. Economically, it is one of the best values for a bowman's dollar. I know I can go off on a mixed-bag African hunt for far less than the cost of chasing a Stone sheep around a mountain. Maybe that's not the right way to look at it, but it's a pretty good point.

I run into more and more people that have gone, or are going to Africa these days. While I only fiddle around with the notion of returning, I'm pleased others are doing it. It really is a "must-do" kind of experience.

A few months ago, during a major trade show, an old acquaintance paid me a visit. "I have finally been to Africa," he declared. "It was just too good a chance to pass up." And of course, he had his well-stocked photo album with him.

We sat as I carefully flipped through the pages. It was a fine collection of extremely good photographs. Each victory, respectfully posed, was "annotated" with an old Bear Kodiak TD and a travel-worn St. Charles back quiver that I know is 35 years old. The photos were structured professionally and perfectly lit in lovely, golden cross light. They were just great, and I told him so. "I tried very hard to set them right, to absorb all the grandeur of the afternoon light." He talks like that, with words like "grandeur" highlighting his conversation. Within his book were dozens of superb prints of the land, the game and the sunsets.

"Have you seen...Oh my!...Of course you have. Aren't the sunsets magnificent, glorious beyond compare?" "Yes," I replied. "They certainly are. Thank you for reminding me."

Maybe I should go back.   ☩

Hammerhead

B efore I moved from California, I spent a great deal of time atop flying bridges and the bouncing bows of sleek, sturdy boats staring across endless purple-blue ocean waters looking for signs. It was almost like hunt'n, only different.

You saw the first birds congregating, wheeling and diving in the distance, and underneath them, with binoculars impossible to hold steady, the frothy white splashes of big fish meeting a brand-new day. Having breakfast. Then you turned and yelled, "Boils, starboard, one-half mile...Hit it!" Then the Gig, Tight Lines, PDQ or a nonchristened fast little skipper of a boat, whatever we happened to be on, turned to the call, surging to that one tiny spot in an ocean of incredible dimension that was the Hot Spot. We slowed, then, stalking, standing at the stern flipping a chum line of live anchovies easing the boat to trolling speed, the chum tantalizing, alluring, as the flashing jigs (blue and yellow were best in my book) skipped in the wake.

Full scoops of bait were broadcast into the wake as the throttles were cut to neutral. The boils came then, up the drifting line of scattered bait fish, and everyone grabbed for a rigged live bait rod and a slippery 'chovy almost frantic to get it into the water where sleek long-finned albacore were blowing up all around the boat. The bait fish would hit the water as your thumb lightly held the reel on free spool, a tug and the reel spun under subtle pressure: Count, don't jerk! One, two, three, four, flip the lever engaging the drag, slack gone. Strike! Uumphh!

Hopefully we could hold the school. The secret was to keep a hot fish hooked up. Pop one off and invariably they left. But when you could hold a school, when the gaff did its work and blood began to drain back into the sea from the deck kept awash and clean by a running hose, when you could keep them there slashing and feeding under the wheeling gulls—that was when the sharks would come drifting in like ghosts.

Mostly they were blue or bonito sharks, not too big, five to eight feet, but big enough to bite a 20-pound longfin in half or shred it to tassels. Once in a while, mostly south into Mexican waters, a Hammerhead, strange, nasty-looking ugly suckers. And there was one time when a long, gray shape slid under the boat, down too deep to really see much more than an eerie suggestion about the size of a submarine, which we thought could have been a Great White. That was long before Jaws, and we knew our boat was big enough.

Of course, the arrival of the sharks ended the fishing. Someone would utter an unkind oath as they felt a new sensation on the line under the deeply bowed rod, a heavier throbbing that ended abruptly leaving nothing but a limp, severed line. We did not think kindly of sharks.

It was during the early days when we would see the twin fins of sharks poking the surface, and we could tell how big they were by the distance between their dorsal and tail—that got me to thinking about getting even.

My bowfishing experience at the time was skimpy. The

first shark, an exercise in stupidity, Lord only knows what I must have been thinking. I wound 100 yards of stout braided line around a shoot-through bow reel, had the presence of mind to use a wire leader connection attached to a solid glass arrow with the biggest fish point I could find and plunked a husky six-footer that slid out from under the boat when we were on a hot school off Catalina's east end. It went well for a moment. The shark left in a hurry as the line whistled from the hooped reel.

Holding the bow one-handed I watched as the line spun from the reel, tightened, cutting the water with a whispering hiss and reached the tag end tied around the handle riser pulling the bow with an arm-wrenching jerk. Adios shark. Farewell trusty bow.

With some trial and error the shark shooting technique was refined. The shoot-through reel maintained with the line running from a sturdy rod and reel around the bow reel to the arrow. The boat rod's reel engaged on a very light drag, free spooling created drastic overruns if it wasn't tended at the shot. Fifty yards of line on the bow reel allowed time to drop the bow and reach the rod in its holder. Some sharks were good to eat. There were days we just went shark hunting. We got some pretty big ones, too, and like any kind of hunting, we hankered for a monster.

It was a Hammerhead off the Coronado Islands. The boat was a 22-footer, and I'm sure it was better than half that length, though now I like to think maybe longer. I was on the bow, hooked up with a yellowtail that still had 50 yards of line on me when it rolled straight below and I was staring right into its dreadfully blank, dead looking left eye. Then it was gone and I had that frustrating feeling that it was going for my fish. It did.

My partners splashed water and chummed to attract it, and it came, three feet between grotesque eyes, maybe more. The arrow struck hard, too far back.

Well over four hours passed before the arrow pulled free. We'd taken turns on the rod as the boat drifted south. I wonder sometimes if that shark is still out there, waiting itself to get even. They say they live for a very long time. I'd like to know. But, as the Sheriff in Jaws suggested: "I'd want a bigger boat!" ▲

Travel
Wise?

I always approach the area with a sense of anxiety, a visceral twinge of foreboding, like, say, going to the dentist for a root canal...I approach them knowing full well the odds are in my favor, statistically, everything should be just fine.

I am a veteran of these things, these places, yet the angst is ever present as I approach and wait. There is always a crowd, a gay, babbling mixture of humanity, kissing, giggling, handshaking, noisy, pressing forward, happy—relieved—to have arrived safely, on time. And so we wait for the buzzer, the bang of the sliding door and the rumbling drone of the conveyor belt in the baggage claim area. That's when I, or we, start to fidget.

They never come off first, our duffel bags and bow cases, tackle boxes or fishing rod caddies. And, of course, in some airports the bow cases won't come off with regular baggage at all, but will be delivered to another area for "Oversized Luggage" (often an inconvenient location) while logo-embossed golf bags of considerable length and heft make the trip amid baby strollers, backpacks, cardboard containers and suitcases, some of sufficient size to hold the worldly possessions of a family of nine.

It doesn't matter where in the terminal the bow cases are delivered, as long as they get there. Sometimes they don't, which provokes a horrible feeling. You're 1,600 miles from home, the outfitter's waiting, camp's three hours south and your bow doesn't show. On two occasions the airline couldn't locate my bow. Now 15 and 20 years later, it's safe to assume they will not. So, in the matter of baggage-claim stress, mine should be easily understood.

I thoroughly enjoy air travel; it's comfortable, fast and safe. With near a million air miles accrued traveling with hunting equipment—many to desolate places—its safe arrival seems as important as your own. In the beginning I traveled with hard cases touted as "Airline Approved". Over time three were trashed. Not destroyed, just all the latches and handles knocked off. In many instances such cases were bulky and inconvenient when bush plane, boat or further horseback travel was required. What's more, their sturdy, locked appearance suggests the containment of valuable equipment (guns), thus piquing the interest of those members of society bent on criminal intent. I sought a better solution.

For 15 years now I've traveled with my bows in a rugged soft case. Holy cow! I can see you all cringe! It's a case built for two bows with an arrow case pocket on the side. It has no fancy camo pattern, is travel-worn, ugly, faded battleship gray and raises no evil-eyeball attention. I rarely pack it with two bows; rather, I pad the extra space with clothing, removing the cable guard, bow quiver and sight so everything's flat. It's soft—when baggage handlers throw it, it lands with a nice, yielding thump and no crashing impact to knock things inside all about—and no latches or handles to tear off. Believe me, it works like a charm.

Another plus to the soft versus hard case method of transport occurs during check-in and baggage inspection. My dowdy case with its full-length zipper is easy to open if requested, meaning no fumbling for keys or stripping tape off fragile latches and no disruption of carefully packed contents.

I fully understand the business of luggage inspection in today's troubled times, yet I've observed some inequities in the process. Occasionally I travel with both bow case and golf clubs. I don't play golf well. If my game produces 15 good shots out of 92 I'm tickled; it's pretty much like the way I shoot a bow. My point is, I've never seen a traveling bag of golf clubs inspected. Oh sure, they probably get X-rayed, but that doesn't hold up the line.

Last year I traveled that way once and stood in line with my three luggage pieces: golf clubs, duffel bag and bow. It was one of those tediously slow lines with time running short. Finally, a lady at the counter pointed my way and said, "Next." I handed over my ticket, photo ID and answered the usual questions: "Has any stranger, etc.?" "No Ma'am!" "Luggage?" she inquired. "Three pieces," I replied and her machine spewed forth the stickum tags. The clubs and duffel sat atop the bow case where she tagged them and swung them to the belt without question. "What's in this?" "Archery tackle Ma'am," which raised a cocked eyebrow. Through Coke-bottle purple eyeglasses the shade of a desert sunset, she looked quite a bit like E.T. "What?" "Archery tackle; you know, bow and arrows."

This pronouncement, 49 times out of 50, is all that's required for clear passage; in the eyes of the FAA, archery equipment does not constitute a threat. "Is it loaded?" "No Ma'am!" "Well," she replied through narrowed purple lids, "I believe we just better check!" A modern compound bow with a caliper release wrapped to it has a pretty lethal look, and I dare say she was on the downside of clueless. "Wait here!" she instructed, and she left me in search of someone of greater knowledge.

Well, I barely made the flight. My luggage did not, which fortunately was only moderately inconvenient. Now as I gear up for another season's travel I'm wondering: Should I sew Titleist emblems on my bow case? ⚵

Chapter 3

The Great Characters

Remembering Pancho

His friends called him "Pancho". I was never sure of the origin of that nickname; his ethnic background was old country European, not Mexican or Hispanic. In his case it fit him pretty well; however, I called him Mister Verzuh, or John. It never seemed right to call him Pancho, though I'm sure he would have thought it was okay. He might have actually liked it.

Pancho was Jay Verzuh's dad. Jay is a close friend of mine, an outfitter in Colorado by profession, though he was once a teacher with a Masters degree in psychology or in some nearly as complicated subject. Now he holds a practical doctorate in all things that have to do with running a hunting operation from A to Z!

Jay and I have hunted together often, but not often enough—that's something we keep working on. Sometimes we have hunted in a guide/outfitter/client relationship. Sometimes we hunt just as two guys who want to set off somewhere together.

Jay called his dad Pancho most of the time, too. Usually when I was with Jay in one of his camps, Pancho was there. They were a team. Pancho was a quiet guy with a catalytic personality. He kept things together. You could learn from him if you paid attention.

Mister Verzuh—Pancho—was a rifleman. He never got around to doing much, if anything, with a bow and arrow. Jay, of course, grew up as a rifleman. Somewhere along the way, his head got turned to bows when it came to serious big game stuff, though both father and son kept their bond with a lot of off-season varmint shooting.

I recall the time I went on my first and only full-blown western prairie dog shoot. As usual, Verzuh style, it was a carefully orchestrated, completely organized affair. Jay had some folks from Remington as clients and a vast chunk of arid real estate to shoot on. Prairie dogs were numerous, far beyond anything I had ever imagined. The shooting was the long-range tack-driving type of stuff serious riflemen love, with a bunch of high-powered, very serious rifle types doing most the shooting. Old John was quietly and politely dead-solid comfortable in his element. I have no firm count of how many rounds we went through in two days, though Jay confided that in the four days it was certainly in excess of 3,000. He had a pretty good idea because he kept all the .22-250 brass. It was enough that I was actually tired of shooting, which is rare. What I do know is even though he must have sometimes missed, I cannot recollect Pancho ever missing a shot!

When I first started bowhunting with Jay, he had a high-powered mule deer place in a lovely stretch of Colorado high country during which may well have been the last prime-time big buck era any of us will ever see. But even then, which was quite a few years ago, it wasn't nearly as good as the days when Pancho was a young man in Colorado. He talked about those days several times. He had watched man's impact on the West, had been part of it actually, like the rest of his generation. Progress meant jobs and a living. It couldn't be helped. He once told me, "Men like you, Jim, and Jay, will have to fight hard to keep what's left."

There was a lot about Pancho that reminded me of my dad: Each had seen the "glory days" in their respective parts of the country. My dad was a South Dakotan who grew up in the middle of the pheasant phenomenon and watched autumn skies and prairie potholes literally solid with waterfowl. He carried a shotgun cradled in his arm as comfortably as Pancho's cheek snuggled against his used, worn rifle stock. I imagine that my dad's exposure might have been a bit more vivid in terms of the crunch of civilization. Southern California, where he reared me, went down the drain at a much faster pace than most places, though Colorado wasn't far behind!

Jay and I talk about our dads. Sometimes it's a little hard, more so for Jay because Pancho didn't leave all that long ago. It takes awhile for the pain to turn into memories. Last September, we were elk hunting a bruiser of a bull, 360 probably, with a serious attitude about possession. He had 49 cows and intended to keep every one. "Now Pancho," Jay said, "would be in here looking to nail one of those fat, dry cows."

"He liked 'em, huh?" I replied.

"Pancho's kind of elk. Sweet and tender," said Jay.

"That's sort of like my wife," I said. "She's really partial to tender elk steaks. Hell, the last one I killed was tougher'n its antlers. She told me to kill a great, old big one for me, or a tender, fat young one for her. She and Pancho would have gotten along."

"Well," Jay said, stuffing the wrappings of his candy bar into a pocket on his pack, "everybody got along with Pancho. If we do this right, we'll get a chance at one or the other."

He almost did it right on that big boy. It was one of those neat situations when you get just close enough with the right kind of cover and wind, pushing hard at the bull's back side as he dogged his cows to turn his instincts around unnaturally. Jay pressed hard, the bull got ticked off, then everything happened too fast. I nocked an arrow and scrambled for good cover, and Jay backed up chirping cow talk.

Damn! There he was, at 15 yards, growling and snot-blowing mad, with me looking for any kind of good shooting hole when the wind shifted. He was very mad, and not at all dumb. A snootful of us sent him packing. Down on our knees on the steep sidehill, drained and breathing in jerky, frustrated gasps, we just looked at each other trying to grin. In all of bowhunting there is nothing as good as a close encounter with a very large elk.

We pressed again the next morning under a sky that promised

all the crazy, nasty things western mountain weather can do to you in September. It started out okay, then fizzled to not very good. It was the last morning, and time was running out. The bull answered defiantly, enough to establish location, traveling fast and not about to be suckered again. We scrambled to catch up and caught a kind twist of fate. Making a zigzag through the timber, we froze. A lagging cow was traveling too slowly. She was sleek, round, broadside and 30 yards downhill. The little Hoyt Spectra went "thump," and the arrow said "chuuunk!"

Mid-November. Three months later. A cozy old farmhouse in Iowa. Long tree stand day. Outside the weather has turned sour. I'm cooking. The house is warm and friendly. The table is set, and the gravy is bubbling. The round steak is perfect. The wind slams the door behind my weather-beaten buddy.

"What are we hav'n?"

"Pancho's elk."

"God, he'd love it!"

"Yes, yes he would." ⟁

Fred's Bow

C harles MacKenzie Kroll is a colorful, kinda crusty descendant of Scot's ancestry whose bowhunting accomplishments have gone largely unheralded. Charlie is the son-in-law of the late, great, legendary Fred Bear, my personal, all-time hero.

It was on the occasion of the 2001 Pope & Young Club Convention–its 40th anniversary–last spring where I greeted Kroll with my customary salutation; "Ahh, MacKenzie!" "Aye Laddie!" he responded through his rusty red and white-flecked, fancy beard and crinkly friendly smile whereupon he handed me a picture with the annotation "Jim Dougherty, Grousehaven '86" on the back.

It's a black and white photo of me sitting on a log in the Michigan woods holding a bow; Fred Bear's personal bow with which I was hunting: it opened a flood gate of memories of The Man, The Time, and The Bow.

Grousehaven was Fred's Michigan hunting camp, a sprawling, wonderfully, comfortable place. Fred loved Grousehaven with deep-seated affection, though not so much for the hunting in the sunset of his years but rather the companionship and camaraderie of good customers and friends. Being invited to Grousehaven was a very special thing; I was fortunate to be included several times.

On a chilly, blustery afternoon in the fall of '86, Fred and I sat alone before a fire just talking. In a corner, near at hand leaned his strung bow, his patented Kodiak TD with four arrow Snap-On quiver loaded with his distinctive yellow and red fletched arrows; three Razorhead tipped, one blunt. I asked his permission to pick it up and pull it. "You're left hand-ed, take it out and shoot it," he responded. "Better still, take it hunting if you like, it doesn't get out much any more," he added with a grin. "Be careful," he said as I headed for the door, his eyes all a-twinkle, "Don't embarrass it."

I shot it that afternoon on the practice range, and golly it felt sweet. It didn't pull very heavy, maybe 50 pounds; at near-ly 85 years Fred had naturally cut down from a lifetime of adventurous bowhunting drawing 65 pounds, or more. At home I had several Bear bows Fred had sent me over time autographed with his favorite hand written sentiment: "Happy Hunting Jim Dougherty...Fred Bear" And on his own bow flex-ing smoothly to my will was likewise hand written: "Happy Hunting Fred Bear...Fred Bear."

The following morning walking quietly to my spot, I was filled with a magical feeling of exhilarating anticipation as his bow hung lightly in my hand. Ahead, three flashing whitetails vanished into the gloom of early morning, the quiet punctuat-ed by a doe's blowing warning. I sat in the stand holding the bow on my lap, most often I hang mine close at hand, but in this treasured hunt I felt a strong need to hold it. Two yearlings came by about an hour after I'd been there, very close, very small, and not worthy of The Bow. Later a spike that was tempting, I even raised it and started some pressure, but no! I had a deep, compelling need to shoot a deer with Fred's bow. Though any deer was legal fair game, I controlled my emotion-al yearning. "Plenty of time," I told myself, "but he better not pass by very often!"

Grousehaven was thick with fox squirrels in a variety of interesting color phases, some pure black; I coveted one of those. In Oklahoma where I come from, they're only the standard rusty red. Near to "getting down time," an inky black model ran up an adjacent tree and proceeded to scold me, straight on offering a target mark the size of a silver dollar: 20 yards. I eased the blunt to the string as he chattered and smacked him dead center! Walking back to the lodge I stroked another off a stump even further. Embarrass Fred's bow?... not hardly. I was feeling pretty darn cocky!

The following evening in came a buck, a branch antlered six pointer feeding in careless unconcern. I knew in an instant I would shoot, yet, as I made ready, shifting my position and raising The Bow, there was unusual trembling in my legs and a strange thumping to my chest. I missed him! Barely 20 yards right over his back. Darn, what a klutz! In recounting the event, Fred found it very, very funny.

In April of '87 I got a long note from Fred that ended: "Let us know if you have a special time for a return engagement at Grousehaven in October. I'll even string up my bow if you want to try again. Could even shoot a deer for you if you are really hungry. Have Fun...Fred." I couldn't go that season, figured I'd make the next time. But, Fred was gone by the fall of '88...there wouldn't be a next time.

I remember a statement he made the day we sat before that flickering fire. He said he knew he was living on borrowed time. I'm forever grateful I was able to share some of that borrowed time, borrow his bow, and that Charlie Kroll brought me the picture.

A Day
In
The Life

I'm pretty certain that most archery hunters who have hunted with a good outfitter would say that outfitting is the epitome of the good life. After all, what could be better than earning one's living in the great outdoors with all that wonderful full-time hunting and fishing? Well, there wouldn't be much better, if that were the case, but it's not.

Good outfitters share an interesting blend of skills. They run their outfits with corporate efficiency. They are adept at tolerating the worst of people's behavior and revel appreciatively in the companionship of those who understand that a bad turn of weather is not the outfitter's fault. Most are philosophical and romantic at heart, in love with the country and the animals they offer for others and constantly concerned with the welfare of both. What people don't realize is what they give up by taking on the business of outfitting—relinquishing their hunting for the benefit of others. That's a concession I find difficult to make.

Thus, in reality, the life of an outfitter is not at all big bulls and bucks taken each season by his hand. The good outfitters put the clients' dreams on the front burner and rarely, if ever, make use of their own bow. But, as I shall tell you, there are good and well-deserved exceptions to the rule.

In the 20-some years I have hunted with Jay Verzuh's outfit, the protocol is as described: commitment to the clients by outfitter and guides. To be honest, though, I do recall a morning when Jay had his bow in the truck when we ran into a huge covey of grouse, and we would have limited out had we not run short of arrows. One time late in the season we hunted together fully armed in search of a lady elk for winter meat. Relying on my steel-trap mind (albeit a bit rusty on the springs), those are the only deviations I recall.

Outside the responsibilities of his Colorado bailiwick, Verzuh and I have hunted together in Texas, Oklahoma, Kansas and Mississippi. In the course of one such outing last spring, when Jay announced his intention to put in for a deer tag and hunt, I was pleasantly surprised. Particularly so when he outlined his plan not to book his usual contingent of hunters for the first week of the season.

A small group of longtime client/friends would put in for deer tags and await the results of the draw in nail-gnawing anxiety. Those who were lucky and drew would hunt giant mule deer, while the unfortunate would run the camp.

"Unsuccessful" is not a kind word relating to most anything, but that's what was said when I entered the Web in search of my drawing results. No deer tag for me, though others, Jay included, were lucky. I have no problem with the drawing procedure—it seems to be fair—but I believe now that I've fallen into the category where senior citizens should be exempt.

Throughout the summer, as Jay went about the business of scouting and readying camp, he hammered my saddened spirit with emails describing the wondrous bucks he was seeing. Then, just short of my departure for camp, he sent me an email apprising me of my duties. In a nutshell (tongue in cheek), he put me in charge. As I can best recall, it was pretty much as follows:

"Your responsibilities will include making sure all hunters are up by 4:30 a.m. (I had to be up by 4 a.m.) and seeing that everyone's at breakfast on time. You will advise all guides and hunters of where they should go and what they should do. You will make certain twice daily that all transportation vehicles are gassed and assist the cook in anything he requires, including proper care of the garbage. You will run any necessary errands for the cook and see that game taken in is properly tagged and bagged before taking it to town. You will be sure that all hunters are in the right truck before departure from camp. You will make sure that anyone hunting from a tree stand has a safety belt. After their departure you will go to the various scouting points, which you well know, and observe."

Jay's email continued, "If you see an elk, you cannot go hunt it; the same holds true for grouse. At 10 a.m. you will check with the guides to see if anyone needs help and if so, go help. You will do the same at dark. Based on observations, you will formulate the afternoon hunt plans and not take time for a nap. You will at all times, regardless of any problem, maintain the same pleasant smile and attitude you have seen me display for the last 20-odd years, and after I have shot my buck and resume control, you can go look for an elk." Jay shot a buck on the fourth day that green-scored just under 190 points. I ran into big bucks almost every day of the season and never took a shot at an elk. It was Jay's turn; I wouldn't have it any other way. ⚓

Chapter 4

The Joy Of Hunting

Another Chance

Since I was a kid, antelope have been one of my favorite big game animals. When we first hunted them in Wyoming, charged with the fire of enthusiastic youth and a carload of ignorance, we knew no other way to bowhunt than to find something and go after it. Age and some experience have refined our methods of pursuit, and we have learned the importance of patience.

I collected an antelope on that first trip to Wyoming, back in the early 1960's, when people who hunted with bows were fewer by far and mostly humored by the landowners on whose doors we knocked. That was before water hole ground blinds, a simple solution to the need-to-get-close problem, became fashionable. The antelope were always somewhere in sight to challenge us to go after them, and we did. It was nothing less than an exercise in humility. However, we were lean, young, and quite a bit tougher then. Crawling seemed logical, and cacti were almost tolerable with the goal only 100 yards away, bedded down, looking off into space, and facing the other direction. It was fun. We thought flaking, sun-scorched noses, lacerated kneecaps, blistered, bloody palms, and dog-tired feet were the logical price to pay. Few victory walks with a game animal have been as euphoric as my trek to the truck the morning I stumbled onto the buck that broke the jinx. Nothing ever smelled quite as good as the strange, sweet odor of antelope. It was my antelope, close to my nose, both arms holding him in place on my shoulders, both hands clutching my beaten, battered, lucky Howard Gamemaster for balance in front.

We changed with the times after that, and the practical application of a shovel, some carefully arranged sage brush, and a bit of baling wire provided roomy, comfortable blinds. Properly dug, with wind direction and the angle of the stark desert sun taken into consideration, they were shaded for reasonable comfort and concealment. Bow shooting antelope became almost a simple thing if you scouted properly for the right water hole.

However, summertime, July and August mostly, is the rainy season in the southwestern desert of New Mexico. It seems unfair if you rely on the water-hole game for a chance at a big pronghorn, the kind that are found here in this country of yucca, sage, sweet grass, and lots of cacti.

As the sun blasts over the horizon, we can feel the growing intensity of its probing rays, and all around us we can see reflections off the scattered silver streaks of lazy puddles caught for a short time in the concrete-hard shallow depressions. The rains came for a week, just days before the season. Flash floods raged down little draws from the raised lava ridges of the not-too-distant malpais. We are in trouble as the odds favoring us taking any waterhole game are dismal.

There are good bucks here, truly big bucks. There are not many of course, just more than I have ever seen anywhere else. There are many more just really nice bucks, mid-to high-70's bucks. Overall, there are not nearly as many antelope as usual, according to the ranch foreman and Ray Milligan, one of my companions who knows this place and has seen it when they are really here. Dave Holt is here with us, fresh from a successful antelope hunt elsewhere, and I tell him he's used up all his luck on the "goats" for this year. The one he took the previous week will make the all-time top 10 in Pope & Young.

Spot-and-stalk antelope hunting is great if you are long on hard work and can bear frustration with a grin without being hung up with some over-stressed need to succeed. I have shot more antelope than I probably need to, but I want to shoot one that is really big.

For two days I scramble in skulking, creeping crawls under the inferno of the broiling New Mexico sun as the need for really-big dwindles. Nice would do just fine. When you get out and really play with antelope, take your time, wait for the breaks and go for it, there is always a chance there will be a chance.

It is a very simple matter to get within easy, point-blank rifle range of antelope on foot. On two occasions I lie a bit inside of 100 yards of antelope that would easily score over 80 inches. I can field-judge antelope reasonably well and much better than I ever seem to do on the whitetails that quite frankly bug me into a big-eyed overestimate. Antelope that score more than 80 are not common in my experience. Antelope that big are worth crawling for.

I crawl through cacti, scrape my shins on the rough lava of the malpais, and lie panting in the heat as thunder storms pass in the distance suggesting shade and moisture while painting the high desert sky with a double rainbow. Sweat trickles onto the lenses of my binoculars and heat waves turn the big desert goats into shimmering, surreal apparitions. The rattlesnakes I meet during the cooling of one late afternoon are pugnacious, nasty creatures that make up in hate what they lack in size. Somewhere in this afternoon with the storms crashing in the distance, I get a chance. It is a reasonable chance. A distinct, unusually widespread buck with horns that sweep back in a long smooth arc, his prongs pointing almost straight up, has been luring me for hours. It seems a folly to dog him at a distance, but I hang on. After all, there is nothing better to do. A fold in the terrain, really nothing more than a slight dip, gives me an edge that I debate even taking. The difference though, for any chance, is to recognize its brief opportunity and seize it. I almost let it slide. The 200 yards seem too far. Surely he will top the next rise while I scramble across the arid red sand in the wide open. However, I do it, sucking the last warm water from the plastic bottle, scuttling half-crouched to the single, landmark bush, then rising carefully with an arrow nocked to peek. I expect nothing, certainly not his back 50 yards away, head down, almost broadside, and nearly perfect.

It is the wind or the arrow that gets me. I play it carefully, back behind his ribs to allow for the drift of the sucking crosswind created by the closing, towering thunderhead. It seems fine at first, but less headway and steerage. The sharpened steel salutes his chest, passing forward of his shoulder, almost touching but not quite. He runs then, in that stutter-step half-trot that antelope have with their rump patches flaring, far to the next rise where we both stand and watch each other until the cooling rain catches me and I turn for the truck.

The white heat of the sun is tempered now by the passing storm's fresh breeze and its downward course to another horizon. It has been a good, tough day, and one to remember, like the one 30 years ago in another summer storm crosswind that came out differently. There are cold drinks at the truck. I get one and watch the sunset and think about tomorrow, about trying it again, about another chance. ⚐

The Rock

I left camp in the fresh cool of a new day, walking slowly along the spiny finger that angled steeply upward to the main ridge of Mt. Orizba. In the distance, far above where low clouds wrapped the peak in a misty shroud, I could faintly hear the bleats and blats of our quarry still a long, hard mile away. I knew that my companions from camp would be pushing slowly upward on other ridges or sneaking carefully through the bottoms of the tight brush-choked canyons, with one eye out for game and the other for temperamental diamondbacks. Our tactic: envelopment of the mountaintop. And I wanted to reach a distant saddle before the rising red-orange orb of the sun burned the clouds away and brought the day's temperature to a broil.

I made it with just enough time to spare. I had chosen a narrow crossing beat deep with intersecting trails pockmarked and powdered dry from centuries of use, a jumbled pile of decomposing rocks formed a good place to hide. I could hear them plainly now as I sucked a deep swallow from my canteen—much closer, they were coming. Slipping three arrows from the St. Charles quiver I nocked one to the string of the Bear Kodiak and laid the others close at hand.

Have you ever bowhunted in a place where it was seriously recommended that you take along at least two-dozen arrows? Not just some extra stuff to plink around with, but full-fledged broadhead-tipped, big-game hunting arrows. Probably not. Most archery hunters have never experienced that sort of opportunity. But I have, along with hundreds of bowhunters in the '60s and '70s. Lots of times, and more often than not, there were rarely any arrows left over when we returned. Are you wondering just where did such a place exist that required heavy-duty hunting quiver overloads, or more importantly, for what? Goats, my friends, Spanish goats on Catalina Island, aka The Rock.

In the early days when the private island's hunting operation first opened you could hunt Catalina over a long three-day weekend for less than a hundred bucks.

Peeking over the rocks from my crouched position I could see them now: a weaving procession of about 50 animals with a dozen or so very big billies intermingled with smaller nannies and kids, a patchwork quilt of assorted colors, some solid, others blotchy two tones, black and white, brown on black, golden palomino, pure white. Spanish goats come in a wide assortment of flavors. The palomino with his wide corkscrew horns drew my eye. He would push 30 inches tip to tip, a dandy old-timer.

The goats crossed through the saddle in a steady walk. Puffs of dust kicked up by their hooves mingled with the strident bleating of the nannies, the deep, guttural baa's of mature billies. Twenty-five yards downhill, the Kodiak strained to the draw, then strummed its vicious tune. Too high! The shaft passed over the golden back, ricocheting into empty space; kiss another one goodbye! Confusion. Another arrow nocked, the golden goat surged forward, hidden behind another, then stopped as the herd milled momentarily.

Second arrow off: thuump! Pandemonium as goats spewed

in all directions, the golden billy in a death dive rolling downhill now through an endless sidehill sea of dangerously nasty prickly pear cactus. Caught in the passion of the moment I searched for another target. There, the big black. Too low! Another shaft gone in a splatter of dust and sparks, it turned him back uphill. Now the sight picture was solid under my eye; the bow canted as my finger touched the corner of my mouth, paused momentarily, then relaxed. Perfect!

Now, I thought, comes the hard part. Ravaged by centuries of erosion brought on by the thousands of goats that systematically were eating themselves out of house and home, the island's ecosystem was in serious decline (the primary reason hunting had been initiated). The arid, crumbly sides of Catalina's steep mountains were hazardous traps to clumsy human feet. Prickly pear armed with toxic spikes blanketed the unstable soil where slipping falls were dreaded and injuries all too frequent. Tweezers, pliers and antiseptic were as essential to our kits as canteens. Claiming fallen trophies was anxious work; retrieving errant arrows was, for the most part, simply ignored.

I have no honest accounting of how many days I hunted Catalina, nor of the number of goats I've taken. And while to some it may seem as overdone, for over the years we took hundreds and hundreds, for the island itself it was an honest necessity. Remarkably beautiful, undeniably mean, for more than 30 years Catalina bowhunting provided marvelous times, and for those who took on her challenge, the ultimate training ground.

It's all over now except for fond memories. The Rock still juts up proudly from the blue Pacific just off the California coast, though hunting has been closed down and precious few goats remain. While hunting was initiated as an effective means of control, newer mind-sets have decreed the goats' total annihilation by other, meaner, less honorable methods. What few goats still exist live precariously now under the pressing thumb of doom. Yet friends of mine who hunted there with me, and now fish the coastline waters beneath her sheer steep cliffs for white sea bass, yellowtail and barracuda, tell me that in the quiet of an early morning, mingling with the rolling sounds of the sea, you can still hear occasional bleats or rumbling baa's drifting down from the mist-covered peaks.

We hope it will always be so. ♠

Departures

The alarm kicked in at 3:45 a.m. This is a dismally dreadful hour no matter what hope-filled adventure awaits, yet somehow, I manage to spring from the bed with enthusiastic, near teenage alacrity. This phenomenon (my teenage years are by now in another solar system) only serves to support my wife's longheld belief that I either have had, or should have, a lobotomy.

By the time I splash, gasp and make it to the kitchen struggling one-legged into my medium weight Thermax underwear the automatic coffee maker has brewed its liquid life-support system and is just ceasing to gurgle and burp, a procedure that sounds (I speculate here) much like a school of trigger fish making love in a blender.

I'm perfectly organized for the mornings, an attitude developed over years (lots) of experience in greeting new days long before it's any day at all. My selected ensemble of camo, warm socks, boots, belt with the lucky buckle and jacket is arranged in order of adornment on the kitchen table. I begin the ritual of garbing myself while simultaneously pressing down the lever of the toaster pre-loaded with two English muffins and failing to notice that it is not plugged in.

Mind you, all of this preparation being accomplished in a hushed atmosphere so as not to disturb my bride: a lady emphatic in pronouncement, and steadfast in assessment regarding the mental state (mine in particular) of anyone who leaps out of bed prior to 6:30 a.m. for any event less than the occasion of childbirth. Therefore, my mood is one of considerate quiet.

My attempted silence, truth be known, is pointless. Wives of more than several decades are not truly asleep when husbands of equal tenure are fumbling around prior to departing for their dragon slaying. No, they are more or less awake cuddling in their Martha Stewart sheets and pillows just hoping you will get done, and outta there. When she yells from the length of the house, "The toaster's not plugged in!" you are acutely aware of this condition.

My pre-hunt nourishment is most often light, like the muffins, cremating now in the toaster, stuck (because their heated, swollen breadth now exceeds the width of the toaster slots) and smoking. I whack the lever ejecting them in a clatter across the counter where they roll like hockey pucks. The strawberry jam is at the back of the fridge behind rows of glass- and plastic-encased condiments and leftovers stacked precariously beneath the foiled remnants of last night's dinner. Retrieving it silently requires the nerves and dexterity of a bomb squad.

Properly toasted muffins have a pleasant texture generating a certain "chewing satisfaction". Cremated muffins, even those garnished with healthy dollops of succulently gooey strawberry jam are, at their best, gritty—something you see doves pecking at alongside the roadway to satiate their gizzards. Time, essential as it was to the hour-plus drive and near mile walk to my cunningly preselected tree stand, obviated browning another batch, besides, I read somewhere that: "Man hunts best when hunger gnaws his belly for it hones his senses and skills to a razor's edge."

As mentioned, pre-departure organization is my forte. My daypack was already stashed behind the drivers side front seat along with the groceries and duffel bag for the weekend. My bow on the workbench in the garage lay in direct route to the truck; gloves, wallet, pocket knife, truck keys and other necessary pocket items are always tucked in my hat. I filled my Go-Cup, laced it with sugar thereby eliminating any possibility of suffering from diabetes in this century. I put the hat on the front seat, the Go-Cup on the dash, cranked the engine, checked the clock and headed back inside for the bedroom.

The ritualistic goodbye kiss, an expression between affection (passion is never an option) and required conduct is accomplished in gloom, any exposed portion of the face being an acceptable target. This is returned (sort of) with a muffled "Gluck", which sounds like a small Canada goose being stepped on. The interpretation being: "Goodby-g'luck-hurry-home-love you."

Back through the house and garage noting in passing it's 4:18 a.m. as I swat the overhead button, duck under the descending door and slip onto the seat: running a tad late and I still have to pick up Pete. Backing the truck out of its shroud of shimmering carbon monoxide air dislodges the Go-Cup that soaks in my new Break Up camo and scalds me (yeah, right there). I decide to ask Pete (he's a judge) if I have a Liability Case against myself.

It's at the corner of 31st and Mingo when it hits me. The lighted intersection illuminates the king cab interior. I peek over the seat: daypack, groceries, duffel, bow. No bow! The bow is in the garage on the workbench where you walked right by the bow in the garage on the work bench. And guess what? The garage door opener is in the garage on the workbench right next to the bow on the work bench. "Arrrgh!" (not exactly, but you got it).

Short of the driveway I cut the headlights so as not to disturb the neighbors who, having suffered pre-dawn disturbances for years would rejoice with news that I have moved to a foreign country. There is not yet the barest suggestion of day to the east. I crossed the dew damp lawn to the far corner of the house where the window, slightly cracked, gives access to my sleeping beauty. I scratched on the screen.

Honey...Hon-ney! "Uuhm, Ghwak?" Honey, I'm Home!　　Ⱥ

Last Play

L ike most everyone I know who loves to hunt elk, I pass the long months between seasons viewing Technicolor dreams of ivory-tipped, six-point bulls bellowing and swaggering in high mountain meadows. Most are so vivid I even hear and smell them. Big bulls turn me on. But, when the time clock is winding down on my annual elk campaign, when it's late in the game—like fourth and nine with five seconds on the clock and the score tied at zero—six-pointers are no longer required. When it's crunch time, any score on the board fills the tag and freezer. Thus, after a sideline visit with my buddy Jay, I elected to sit a stand near Lemonade Spring in hopes of a last second score, an elk hunting field goal if you will.

Sitting stands is not my favorite elk hunting scheme, I much prefer moving around. Perhaps that is because I know I'll be plunked on a stand for most of October through December waiting on whitetails. Carefully sneaking through elk country is my idea of a much better bowhunting time.

The days had been too hot and dry though, poor conditions for sneak hunting, and calling had been double tough with the bulls pretty much shut-mouthed and uninterested. Oh, I'd heard a few languid squeals, but the big boys were mostly kicking back in heavy cover waiting for things to cool down before they heated up. And, too, it was my own fault my tag was still tucked in my daypack. No misses, just a couple of screwed-up stalks and two dumb passes on smallish bulls. Trophy greed usually comes back to bite me in the butt!

My eleventh hour call to sit at the spring made sense. Tree stands in cool glades near water holes and wallows had been paying off all through this hot season. My son Holt and our two buddies Jim Kondos and George Gardner had all taken their very first elk just that way. Leave it to me to be stuck on the wandering approach. I kicked the options around with my outfitter amigo Jay Verzuh in whose camp I religiously spend the better part of each September. We agreed. The sweet gushing water of Lemonade Spring seemed like a good last-minute bet.

There was a long hill on the last three-quarter-mile walk to the spring. It was dry, dusty and warm, and the air was way too thin to hike in very fast. At the top of the grade I shucked my camo shirt and searched my pack for the half-frozen bottle of cold Gatorade. The light southern breeze felt good in the shade. From the top of the hill there is an old ranch road that drifts softly downhill to the Cabin Without a Roof. The road was powdery, cinnamon-brown talcum churned by plodding range cattle, mule deer and elk—my steps sent up little puffs as I walked. There were fresh elk tracks on the old road, and the clean imprints of bear. A sow and a cub had walked here that morning. I always get a visceral knotting feeling walking on fresh bear tracks, and the chances of stumbling right on top of one seem to be about 50-percent in my experience here at Jay's. If I had a bear tag I'd probably never see one. I never have one so usually I stumble onto several. Near the bottom of the road, short of where the old cabin sits was a freshly ripped old fallen log. On a nearby aspen I could see where the cub had shinnied up, the fresh yellow-green scratches stark wounds on its soft chalky bark.

The stand at Lemonade hangs in a century-old pine 30 yards from the spring which gushes from the steep sidehill right onto the road. Where it has eroded the topsoil there is a crystal clear pool in clean-washed rock before it drains down the road to be trampled and muddied by stout free-ranging Hereford who are never too far away. It's really in a canyon with near 60-degree walls—the old road simply cuts a weathered ledge along the east side. On the west side a sheer grassy glade rises through a stand of mature 60-foot aspen before giving way to mixed thick patches of snowberry and scrub capped toward the top by mature growth heavy dark timber. It's a heck of a spot.

Half a dozen sullen cows stared anxiously at me from their sloppy beds in the road as I climbed the last 100 yards. At the base of the tree I slipped into my shirt, snugged the safety belt to my waist and tied my bow to a dangling cord. Reaching for the first step I noticed my watch, 4 p.m., straight up. Last play: game underway.

Facing the tree I hung my bow to the left and struggled to adjust the safety belt with sticky pitch-covered fingers. Fumbling, mouthing silent bad words for forgetting to wear gloves, the thumping of hooves on the road to my right merely suggested the trotting approach of another thirsty cow. A cursory glance nearly generated a stroke! Fifty feet away, nostrils flaring, eyeing the cows with a hostile glare stood a tawny-bodied, real live bull elk.

Not breathing—snugged close to the tree—I managed to pass the bow from left side to right hand and nock a XX75. More silent bad words. My sap-coated left hand stuck in my pants pocket while trying to reach my release.

Then, luckily, for last plays demand some luck, it all came together, the bow storing energy as the bull stepped forward; bolting hard, struck clean by the Thunderhead, racing straightaway, scattering cows, spraying mud, rolling now—stone dead between two pines that bracketed the road 60 yards away.

On the stand, melting down with an emotional overload I glanced at my watch: 4:03 p.m. Game over! ♠

Chapter 5

Strange Happenings

Rack Attack!

This was fun! The young seven-pointer was poised on trembling, spring-loaded legs, his intense stare carefully x-raying the tangled web of South Texas brushland sprawling to infinity behind me. At 50 yards, in the gloom of a dull, misty dawn, his muted gray form had suddenly taken shape, revealed by the contrast of his white throat patch against the drab morning's tangled background. Hunkered in a ground blind that was woven into the twisted form of a gnarly old mesquite and prickly pear, I watched him through the shooting hole. He's a pretty little guy, I thought, picking up the antlers to tickle them again.

He wasn't a shooter, but I was so intent on his reactions to the subtle clicking—the three quick steps he took and the neck-straightening jerk—that I was caught flat-footed by the eight pointer that suddenly appeared on my left. It was one of those damp, quiet kind of mornings that was made even quieter by the sandy loam soil. I finally became aware of the swishing sound through sand and damp grass and shifted my gaze. Ooooops!

South Texas mornings can be like that. When the weather finally cools around mid-December, the muy grandes, as Texas buck-busters are fond of calling big whitetails, begin to range and rumble. Rattling antlers amid the thorny, cat-clawed heavy cover these bucks call home is a traditional hunting method among Tejanos, and there's no other place where it works quite as well. I make it a point to be there when it's happening, but I admit to a fascination with the land as well as the variety of other game, too. While I go there to hunt deer, that's not all that draws me. I like the action that the abundance of wild hogs, javelina, turkeys, coyotes and bobcats commonly provide on a typical South Texas jaunt. As I said at the beginning, it's fun!

The two bucks were staring each other down now. Further rattling tactics were unnecessary; the real thing was smack-dab in my lap. The eight pointer was a slightly better buck, though both were youngsters of equal age sharing the same interests and temperament. In South Texas, cool December days cause deer action to perk up—that's when you need to be there. The seven pointer started forward with an attitude best described as belligerent. Oh boy! I thought. Live decoys.

They circled each other. The seven pointer's ears were laid back, his hackles slightly flaring. If the bucks vocalized threats, I could not hear them. I had the impression that the eight pointer, who had distinctively better antlers, wasn't really interested in a serious rack attack. Not so the pugnacious seven. He lunged suddenly, spiking the bigger deer with a vigorous, ungentlemanly assault on his behind. That did it. They squared off. I imagined the bigger buck exclaiming, "Well now, that tears it!"

It didn't last long; most of the buck fracases I've witnessed seldom do, though obviously there are serious, sometimes deadly encounters between rival deer. Some years ago I found a dead buck, a nice-size deer that had recently died from three nasty puncture wounds to his soft underbelly. I'm sure they were inflicted by another buck that was either stronger, meaner or just luckier. I once shot a buck that only had one eye. I always assumed he had lost the other in a fight, though I really don't know. Before you leap to ignoble conclusions, I took him from the good side, though I didn't know there was one at the time.

Fights to the death are most likely a simple matter of bad luck rather than serious, malicious intent—antlers locked accidentally being the biggest cause. The two before me, wheeling in the sand, strained against each other and, for a fleeting moment, appeared to be truly welded together, only to pop apart with a scraping snap.

As you can imagine it was fun to watch. Nonetheless, all the while, I was keenly keeping tabs on my surroundings in hopes that this true-to-life sequence might toll in a buck worth getting knee-jerking jittery over. Whoops! Abruptly it appeared as though something special was about to happen. The bucks, taking a side-heaving breather between rounds, suddenly snapped their attention to the east, rose to full-alert with ears cocked above hard stares, then spun as one. With twin snorts they dashed away, flashing flagtails high, for the sanctuary of the deep mesquite. To my right I could hear the soft thumping of hooves. Muy grande comes, I thought, gripping the Defiant a little firmer, glancing at the arrow, checking the distance from point to shooting hole. No time to make a noisy mistake. I peeked.

Damn! My grande venado dream materialized into a trundling grundle of wild hogs. While I have often seen deer and javelina fraternize, albeit grudgingly, it seems that deer seldom tolerate the presence of wild hogs. Certainly my two boisterous bucks wanted no part of them, but I did. It was one of the reasons for being there—action—one of those extra opportunities, a bonus. I took it.

Looking the snuffling, shuffling band over, I selected one with all the succulent dimensions for a perfect fit above a glowing bed of mesquite coals on the old camp grill. I laced his chunky ribs with a Thunderhead 100. My rationale: The pigs scared the deer, I scared the pigs. Fair's fair, and the barbecue was delicious.   ⚙

Mistaken Identities

F unny how the mind sometimes misinterprets what the eyes see. I was slipping along the downwind side of a long sage-covered ridge speckled here and there with little stands of pine and a smattering of young aspen. It had rained during the night, a hard rain accompanied with rolling thunder as the clouds beat up on each other. There had been lots of lightning, the white-hot, crackling kind that blows trees apart and starts serious fires. Just a half mile away, on a parallel ridge, a 200-year-old pine stood, split from crown to base, the burning core of its heart exposed as it smoldered blue plumes and began to die in the fresh dawn.

My plan was to move quickly but carefully below the crest of the ridge for half a mile, then cross it and work back up into the crosswind on the other side. The opposite slope had heavy stands of mature aspen and solid patches of lush, succulent snowberry. At the head of three different draws were shady nooks that bucks would move into as the day heated up—altogether a perfect piece of spot-and-stalk mule deer country.

The freshly washed air was saturated with the sharp smell of pine and sage, mixing with the faint scent of smoke from the mortally struck pine. I was completely caught up in the joy of it, of being there sneaking along the ancient rain-softened cow trail through the waist-high sage. But then I saw the spiders. Huge spiders. Upside-down spiders with thick fuzzy brown legs pointing at the sky waving along the horizon uphill to my left.

In the flicker of a millisecond what the corner of my eye had seen was transferred to a four-color billboard on the portion of my brain that attempts to interpret, sort and deal with the image. The message was: Tarantulas. Huge. Upside down. Whoa!

Weird? No question. But that was the pictured message. Of course it couldn't be, at least I hoped it couldn't be as I scrunched in the sage for a better, more direct look. My spiders were there alright; the velvet-encased tines of four mule deer bucks protruded just above the tops of the sage 50 yards away and they did appear to be the dancing hairy appendages of some inverted giant arachnids. I shook the surreal apparition from my apparently short-circuited head and set about the task at hand. About an hour later I knelt beside one of the bucks, the last in the line of four that had fed too slowly on a meandering course through the blue-green sage and allowed me to get too close. I ran my hands over the length of the soft velvet-clad tines and savored the moment.

Visionary misinterpretations are common enough when we hunt. The gloom of predawn conjures up all sorts of things. Broken stumps become bears—straining eyes and wishful thinking seem to give them life and make them move. The changing angle of afternoon sunlight always impresses me with its illusions—a hot spot on the white bark of a sycamore: Is that the throat patch of a buck? But these are common, almost expected, illusions brought on by changing light on rocks, logs and blackened stumps. They are nothing like the illusion of the cow.

I was in a tree stand near the bottom of a dark, cool canyon guarding the trail to a well-used wallow complex. The grass in the bottom was thick, juicy green, and with the wallow fed by a gurgling spring it was a natural gathering spot for stocky range cattle, as well as elk, to water, generally ignoring their distant cousins. Mule deer are more standoffish. There were perhaps a dozen snuffling, moaning cattle present at the time, and while I dislike their presence in a hunting spot, I learned long ago that when you hunt in the West, like it or not, they're just part of it.

An hour before dusk as a cooling chill settled in the canyon, a bull elk bugled behind me. He sounded pretty close! Then I could hear the birdlike chirping and soft mews of elk cows and calves. I had to stand up and face the tree, part of the plan; when the elk came they would come from below, then pass on my right on their way to the spring at 15 yards. It's a cool setup. The huge pine whose girth required an extra length of chain to hold the tree stand provided ample cover. I waited and watched, peering into the darkening aspen grove with my eyes straining in anticipation of the first glimpse of the elk herd. A snuffling, shuffling interruption from behind provoked a quick reactionary turn of the head. My cursory glance identified the reddish bulk of an approaching range cow. I turned to resume my peeking vigil.

Even as I turned, the picture book in my mind was cranking out funny signals. The technicolor billboard flashed, relaying and replaying the image just seen, clanging into focus with an electrifying jolt. Eyes to brain: Check this out! There on the screen, waddling straight toward the base of my tree was the biggest cinnamon-red bear in all of Colorado. I spun back so quick I damn near threw my back out of whack.

The motion caused the bear to pause and examine my presence. He did so in a deliberate manner, like a large black bass contemplating a fingerling bluegill. He even licked his lips. He was the biggest black bear I have ever seen and I have seen a train load. I wished he'd turn back into a cow.

Our meeting was nervously brief. Watching me over his shoulder he ambled off down the trail toward the elk, a shambling, rolling, huge hulk of a bear. I guess he boogered them, because the last hour passed in slow, totally inactive silence. I wondered if he'd eaten them all.

Of course, I had to walk out of there in the inky black, down the same trail the bear had taken. I saw him, too, in the gloom, coming back. There was no place to go. I was even starting to nock an arrow when the billboard clicked in. Whew! It was just a cow.   **A**

Spoiled Day

It happened a year ago. This year it happened again. It was early spring this time with some positive signs of green in evidence. Catkins were beginning to dangle, and plump young buds were swelling under the pressure of new leaves and flowers anxious to emerge. It was a warm day, pleasant under a clear, cloudless sky with gentle south winds. I figured I'd swing by my trailer to make sure everything was in good shape after the winter's pounding, then drive to a spot where I could take a long walk to collect the first one. I chose the long way so I could cover more ground looking for turkey sign along the way. I'd head north, drop into a major drainage, wander through that, go east uphill to the ridge, then go south to the point of collection.

With spring in the air, turkeys were much on my mind. Collecting the first API Twister tree stand from the gnarled old oak on the crest of the ridge was just part of the reason for making the trip. I found plenty of turkey sign in the bottom; the fresh tracks of two big toms cast in the mud wound my turkey hunt'n crank even tighter. My mood was pleasantly tuned as I climbed to the ridge.

I should have pulled the Twister right after deer season, but I had others to contend with and just let it ride. After all, it was in a safe place on private land. I figured the camo-covered foam seat would likely be in tatters—fox squirrels seem to like to chew them up to stuff in their nests—but if that was the case, it could easily be fixed. I was right. The seat was a mess. The remnants reminded me of a stale yellowed angel food cake that had been tossed in a shredder. Twenty yards away, I spied pieces of foam protruding from a hole in the trunk of a dying old oak. That was okay; the bushy tail had entertained me often during deer season. I pulled the stand and "Stackin' Stiks", then I humped cross-country to the truck.

The drive off the hill to the next spot was hellish—a steep, washed-out rocky track that I'm sure makes my old truck want to scream. It can't, of course, though it groans and creaks over its 103,867 miles in metallic wearisome complaint. At the bottom where the rotten road flattens, six whitetails stood in nervous confusion, their nap interrupted by clattering rattle. I can see they're all bucks through the 10X42s; their bulbous new antler growth has begun to take shape. Their white flags dance and wave as they dash across the prairie. I'll see them again when I scout through the summer.

The next stand location was in a meandering low bottom that's brush-clogged and nasty in the fall. As I walked in, the new greenbriers snatched at my jeans, the draining ground was tacky and mucky and the air was musty-damp from decomposing leaves. In winter when beavers dam the creek, the bottom backs up knee-deep in water; that's a haven for mallards. On cold, north wind-swept days it's a fine place to be with a friend, a few shotguns and a sackful of decoys.

I have shot several deer in this place, though not one last season. A good buck was using it, but we never crossed trails. His rub line was still brightly visible on wrist-thick persimmon, and a 10-inch cedar wore deep scars from fall thrashing. The stand was—or should have been—in a huge, sprawling Bois d'

Arc tree at the edge of the creek. It's a fine old tree. In the fall it is heavily laden with softball-sized yellow knobby-veined fruit that remind me of alien heads in a sci-fi action thriller. The squirrels come to them, then the deer after the fruit has fallen and lain on the ground for a while. Our deer seem to like them late in the season, though I think maybe more out of necessity than preference. I've been to many places where they pay them no mind.

Being intent on where I stepped and reading all the tracks—deer, coyote, raccoon, armadillo and rabbit—I didn't realize the stand was gone until I was very nearly there. No handy strap-on ladder sections, no Alum-I-Lok 100... just a bare empty tree, with the sheared padlock chain a linked heap at my feet.

My pleasant mood soured as I sat on a stump angrily disgusted. As I stated at the beginning, that's twice in two years. I wonder what possesses some people to steal? Hunters stealing from one another seems especially rotten to me. I wonder if those who stole my stands recognize themselves as crooked common thieves, that if caught and convicted they could be branded as felons? Being labeled a felon is a bad tag to wear. Do these perpetrators realize what low-life, cheating scumbags they are? Probably not!

Tree stand thievery is commonplace today. There's precious little we can do to protect our stands against trespassers, bolt cutters, chain saws or axes. The scene of the crime sure spoils a fine day.   ▲

Lucky, Lucky

Four wheelers. Four by fours. Quad-Runners. ATV's. Whatever you call them, they are marvelous, rugged machines with a go-almost-anywhere attitude. Used properly, they're a wonderful tool. I'd love to have one. However, as a practical matter, I do not. They're pretty expensive. Besides, when I occasionally express the desire and investment required in the presence of my wife, the comment is met with a rolling-of-eyes look she developed somewhere back in the late '50s and has since carefully honed. The Look is always supported by what she considers sound logic, as in "Dear, we have no place to put it!" Suggesting that her treasured early last millennium Sedan DeVille might be parked in the drive in order to garage a Quad Runner would fly like a brick. "And," she continued, "I don't want you on one. Remember what happened last year? You're lucky you weren't killed!" Reflecting on last year certainly gives strength to her position.

Last year got off to a pretty fair start. Late August found me in Jay Verzuh's bowhunting camp settling in for the season.

I shot the buck mule deer that really wasn't a buck (regardless of the 5X5 rack on its head) the third day. The whatever it was/is deer collapsed at the bottom of what I now refer to as "Morph Basin", mere yards from a sheer drop-off. That was the good part. The bad part was the steep three-quarter-mile uphill pull necessary to retrieve it. We could have quartered and backpacked it, but Colorado law dictates that evidence of sex is required on carcass pieces. Considering this deer's sex was something of a question—one end compared to the other if you will—taking it out intact seemed best.

Verzuh keeps several four-runners for such chores. After carefully studying the terrain, Jay decided how he could get close to it on his big green Polaris 600. Maneuvering the sturdy machine to within 50 yards and returning heavily laden was a ticklish task. The skill Jay displayed zigzagging the precariously tilting machine across the treacherous side hill was an exhibit of expertise witnessed with thanks and appreciation. What he accomplished in an hour saved a day's back-breaking labor.

I claim no such four-wheeler expertise. My experience with them is limited mostly to dirt roads and trails, not much cross-country stuff, but I'm experienced enough to know that while they are wonderfully designed to go nearly anywhere, they can be tricky and fickle, be it smooth road or cross-country, as the following will illustrate.

Several afternoons later, I dropped Judge Pete off near a water hole stand a big bear had been frequenting. I told His Honor I would see him after dark and chugged up the canyon on the old logging road, comfortably seated on Jay's mighty 600. Although it had rained the day before, the trail was now powder dry except for a few shaded spots that were still a bit slick. I parked on top of the last hill I intended to ride. From there, I would walk a mile to one of my favorite afternoon elk spots.

The afternoon passed quietly. A cow elk and calf came to the spring, as well as a forked-horn mulie. As shooting light faded to dusky gray gloom, I gave up for the day and headed back to the four-wheeler. By the time I tethered my daypack and bow to the front rack, it was black dark. The piercing beam of the headlight illuminated a porcupine at the crest of the hill. It shuffled away as I pushed the gear lever to low range and eased off. It is said that in moments of sheer anxiety or terror one's life flashes through the eyes of the mind. Halfway down the slope, the machine began to slide sideways. Just as the left front wheel dropped in a rut, I experienced a blink of anxiety but no terrified review of my life. At my age, there is hardly enough time!

There is something discomforting about waking up, head pointing downhill, with 500-plus pounds of mechanical monster atop your left leg while the right one's pointing skyward. A deep breath indicated something amiss with my ribs, and my pinned leg felt strange, though not broken. The Polaris was on its left side crossways to the downhill slope, and it settled firmly on my thigh. For 45 minutes I kept pushing, lifting it up mere fractions each time, straining mightily with every push to pull free. Lying there in the still darkness, out of breath, exhausted, cold in the mud, staring at a sky full of stars and the blinking high lights of a westbound airliner, I knew I was lucky, it could have been much worse. Several times, I shattered the quiet with a hard yell for Pete. No answer!

Finally, my leg was just stuck in the boot. I managed to unlace it. When I finally reached a standing position I ached all over, and the hot rush of adrenaline had ebbed to cold shivering shock. I threw up. Eventually, I hobbled down the old road to where Pete could hear me. "Leave your stuff there and come up here," I called. "You got something down?" "Yeah, I got something down!" It wasn't quite what he figured!

Luck, good and bad, plays a role in many things we do. It was bad luck the machine tipped over—it really wasn't its fault or mine—and truly good luck the damage to my leg, though severe, wasn't worse. I still covet a four-wheeler, an admission that brings forth The Look—Luckily, I'm still here to see it. ⚐

Chapter 6

Other Critters

The Fever
Of Fall
Gobblers

If you happen to run into someone who knows me, they
will undoubtedly tell you that each spring, about mid-
March, I slip a gear. Some will claim it's nothing less than
a totally stripped transmission.

"Otherwise, if we ignore the spring thing," they might say,
"Dougherty is a reasonably competent, generally okay sort of
guy dedicated to his family, bowhunting, and his archery business. However, in the spring, he has turkey fever," they will add
in the same hushed voice used for passing on information
about a terminal ailment.

Turkey fever has a far greater capacity for screwing up an
ordinary mind and body than a simple disease. Anyone can
contract something terminal; only the fortunate get turkey
fever.

Turkey fever began near the first of April, ran its course
filled with sleepless nights and daytime gaunt-eyed pursuit in
quest of the cure. It ended with perpetrators of the ailment
wrapped in their freezer bag shrouds awaiting final dispensa-

tion, and the patient, 10 pounds lighter, gearing himself to resume a "normal" life.

However, afflictions such as fevers are known to be tenacious buggers that fight for survival with an intensity equal to the efforts designed to destroy them. And so, it is with a heavy heart that I inform you of the existence of a new, equally virulent strain of the fever. While it may not be as debilitating as the spring variety, it promises to have a pronounced effect on my ability to think clearly during deer season. That, in and of itself, is cause for serious concern. As a result of being severely overexposed late last October, I have fallen victim to fall turkey fever.

The prognosis is fair. Hopefully, it will be harder on the turkeys than myself.

Although I knew the disease was common within some circles of my acquaintance, attempting to fill all my fall whitetail tags provides a pretty full plate. The Oklahoma Department of Wildlife Conservation made the potential for contracting the disease all the greater when it established a fall bow season for turkeys running in tandem with the first half of the archery deer season. What that did, for which all Oklahoma archery hunters are sincerely grateful, was give us about six weeks to fling arrows at turkeys if we were so inclined. I have never been one to pass up a chance at a legal fall turkey if an opportunity happened along. On the rare occasions over the years this occurred, two birds went home with me. One was collected on a beautifully arching 50-yard shot with a travel-worn recurve. That it was not the turkey I'd focused on is meaningless information.

Generally, in establishing the whereabouts of fall turkeys, I have been content to carefully note the age and sex of the birds in the flocks, catalog the mature toms in my mind for the spring wars, and go about my pressing deer-hunting business. Should one stupidly stand about, I launch. That hasn't happened very often. These encounters did not result in ague or feverish nights until last season when I met the Wild Bunch.

The Wild Bunch was a flock of jakes that in the month of

October numbered 23 birds. They began to frequent one of my pet deer areas in which I had never seen a single turkey track, much less a full flock during five years of hunting this location. The mast crop had hardly enough acorns to sustain the old male fox squirrel whose winter den tree sits 40 feet from my stand. I don't know why they were there; the deer certainly were only transients. It was an unusual season, the presence of the jakes making it even more so. I started thinking about the turkeys pretty hard; began talking about them at home. They were serious conversations, mostly to myself. The wife took note of my glazing eyes, felt my forehead, and made reservations to California to visit her mother and brothers. Curbside at the airport she gave me one of those tender kisses mothers reserve for a sick child.

The jakes had infected me. It was time to bone up on fall tactics, pick out the right diaphragm call for perfect Kee-Kee runs, make the proper equipment adjustments, and gear-up mentally. Like the spring fever strain, the only cure is pursuit. By Friday afternoon I was ready. It was time to engage.

Saturday morning was clear and cool. I lay in wait amidst the tangled remains of a downed oak some 75 yards from my tree stand. The first thing to appear was a chunky buck—the meat and potatoes kind—that walked right by the stand. I would have shot him if I were there, but I wasn't. The turkeys came right on schedule, though not right for a shot from my blowdown ambush. Time for Plan A.

Plan A for fall turkeys is a tactic commonly referred to as the scatter. Scatters are effected by instilling panicky mass confusion in the turkey flock. Shotgunners in the fall accomplish this with a foot charge supported by considerable yelling and the rapid discharge of their three-inch 12-gauge magnums. In my break up, I performed steps one and two, step three seemed inappropriate. My bow is not very loud, and I have been taught never to shoot an arrow straight up. The scatter was superb.

Step four of Plan A, after the birds have been scattered, is to seek cover, regain both breath and composure, then, after a settling down period, begin calling. For perfect results you should begin calling just before the real birds think it is time. This, of course, is a crap shoot. It's not the end of the world if your timing is off, just perfect when it's right. Mine was impeccable. I was answered immediately from all quarters. In a matter of moments the woods were filled with the squealing, breaking yelps of adolescent gobblers mixed with the staccato tattoo of churning feet scurrying through the ankle-deep leaves. Bobbing heads on sleek bronze bodies were bearing down from every angle. General Quarters!

Young turkeys, turkeys of the year, are not super sharp. While we have a tendency to accord the mature three-year-old tom the cunning of a cat burglar mixed with the brain of a rocket scientist, first-year fall turkeys are really pretty stupid. The only thing dumber is a guy in a fumbling hurry trying to shoot one with an arrow. Bows, it should be pointed out, are much more unwieldy to maneuver under these conditions than shotguns. My first arrow pulled feathers from an incomer that turned inside out when he saw me draw. After the shot, he stood 15 feet away to watch me load. Not long enough. I swung on a second bird that walked by and gobbled, centering a 1½-inch sapling. Given six shots, I couldn't hit that sapling again on purpose. The third bird (thankfully, the last as they scurried away again), from which I cut a tail feather, went straight into geophysical orbit.

That however, does not matter. What matters is the exposure resulting in a new strain of the disease. Now if anyone asks about me, they'll be advised, "Oh, Dougherty. He's a weird one—turkeys you know!" ♠

Varmint
Memoirs

The bonfire had run its course. All evening it had been devouring a pile of crisp-smelling cedar logs, reducing them finally to a bed of glowing embers. Everyone scrunched up closer, with their warm fronts and chilled behinds. The night was clean and cold, a vast black canopy stretching forever studded with a zillion icy stars.

The coyote sounded incredibly lonesome. His two quick yips were followed by a long and pitiful yowl. It was a mournful call trailing off unanswered into the empty Texas night. His cry hushed the murmur of quiet campfire conversation. Each man paused to listen for a moment as the call stirred private thoughts of wild places and wilder things.

Someone bent to the blackened coffee pot that was snuggled near the glowing embers. The movement brought everyone back to reality and the brief, simple spell was broken.

"Did you ever shoot a coyote?"

The speaker was a young easterner hunkered closely to the coals with his palms extended. His eyes glittered in the firelight. His face was smeared with camo paint, heavy on the black, and he reminded me of a raccoon. He was big into face paint and not much on washing it off. I had been around him for two days and still didn't know what he really looked like.

"Yes," I replied, "I have shot some coyotes."

"Jim invented coyote calling," said one of my old amigos from across the fire.

"That's not true," I replied, "but I did get on the train pretty early in the ride. We sure used to have a great time varmint calling, and I spent a lot of time with the guys that really did invent it: Wayne Weems, the Burnham brothers, Jack Cain, and Lou Mossinger. They're some of the best all-around hunters I've ever met. It was a lot like this: We'd camp out on the desert for three or four days at a whack, hunt all day, and most of the night too where night calling was legal."

The face-painted youngster stood and stretched, turning his chilled backside to the fire. "We have some coyotes where I come from now, but never did before. No one had ever heard of a coyote 10 years ago. I've never seen one but I've heard them; I'd really like to get one."

"Coyotes are neat," I offered. "They take a lot of abuse, properly so sometimes, but mostly they get a bad rap. The thing I like most about them is their incredible adaptability. That and the fact that the best time to hunt them is in the winter months when everything else is over and done. We hunted coyote, bobcat, and fox the hardest during January and February. That's when they make the best trophies too, because the pelts are at their prime."

"You call bobcats, too?"

"You bet. They're easier than coyotes really, because they're not nearly as sharp as coyotes. I don't know how many I have seen come in straight downwind. Coyotes hunt with their noses as well as their eyes, and you need to thump them before they get on the downwind side or it's bye-bye Jose! However, cats will sneak in on you and take their time doing it. Usually they will spook once they see you, but not always. I have seen them do some stupid things. I have seen entire quivers of arrows shot at a sitting cat, and a few magazine loads of high powers, too. One day years ago I called up a cat for a guy who had one of those new Bear snap-on bow quivers that holds eight arrows. He shot the first arrow at about 20 yards and the last one at somewhere around five or six feet. I guess that was his range because he got him with his seventh arrow. It was a big cat, one of those long-legged desert cats with gorgeous spots and a snow-white belly. I've never seen anything like that happen with a coyote. I've seen lots of gray fox that were almost as suicidal. One jumped in the bed of a pickup one night with three of us standing in there calling. The tailgate was down, and he landed in there with a pretty serious attitude and didn't seem at all interested in leaving. About the same time a horned owl made a very low pass. It was pretty lively before things got straightened out. There have been several incidents with guys I know who actually got jumped on by foxes and bobcats.

"Varmint calling prompted our first thoughts of some form of cover scents. I remember that Jack Cain was the one that started Circe Calls, using garlic oil in an attempt to beat the downwind coyotes. Back then there wasn't a big scent market to speak of except for a few trapping supply houses that offered some really vile concoctions that were awfully tough on stomachs early in the morning. We played around with whatever we could find and settled on some rabbit scent from a dog training supply house. We used it, but I believe playing the wind was the true secret to success, just like it is for whitetails. You might confuse the youngsters a bit, but the old-timers, be they bucks or coyotes, are seldom fooled by our human gimmicks.

"The tricky part is learning about the critters well enough to put them where you want them. It's just simply a matter of applied experience: You learn as you go and improve in the process. When we first started we made all kinds of mistakes. Learning where to call is much more important than being a good caller, and if the truth be known, the technique required for good varmint-calling success is pretty simple. It's a lot easier than turkeys or ducks. The nice thing about it is that there are plenty of critters wherever you are, and generally speaking, there's a year-round opportunity at most places, plus a general willingness by landowners to let folks get them. Remember, varmints, especially coyotes, are usually considered to be bad guys. Being pretty good at clobbering coyotes has opened a lot of gates for me when it came time for bowhunting deer or shouldering my shotgun."

Both the youngster and I extended our cups to the sizzle of the coffee pot, then settled back to cradle the warmth in our cold hands. A light breeze had picked up from the north and someone prodded the fire and tossed in a fresh log. On the distant ridge the lonely coyote wailed his song again.

"You know," I mused, "the best thing about varmint calling is the unexpected. You can never be sure what might come or what will happen. The last black bear I shot came to a harsh jack rabbit-voiced call in a spot I thought would be good for coyotes. I had a bear tag in my pocket and a broadhead on the string, but I sure wasn't expecting a bear!

"I'll tell you what. The weather's right and the timing's good. After we deer hunt in the morning, say about nine, we'll do a little sashay around the ranch. I won't guarantee you'll get a coyote, but there's a darn fine chance you will get a chance. It's bedtime, let's sleep on it."

It was cold away from the fire, and the night felt bigger and blacker. On the distant ridge the coyote wailed again. This time he got an answer, then another. "Yeah," I thought, "he'll get a chance." ⚲

Wild Boar

The first wild hog that I ever took with a bow wasn't much; no glamorous tusks graced his pointed snout. I'd guess that he field-dressed around 60 pounds. Still, as I tiptoed the last few yards, seeking the perfect shot for my 55-pound recurve, all sorts of scary notions ran through my mind. After all, this was the first "dangerous game" I'd experienced, and my head was full of the fearsome tales that surrounded their pursuit.

At close range, the snuffling grunts of the foraging hog did little to calm my twitching pulse. I suppose then, in teenage innocence, that I fully expected a charge. When the moment was right, I grew calm enough to loose an arrow that sent him packing in a rush. In my mind, I can still see a runamuck black, mud-coated bowling ball bowling a perfect strike through the lacework of tangled scrub oak. At the trail's end, his inert form had somehow shrunk from the grunting monster that I had stalked.

Let's get it straight from the get-go. All wild pigs, regardless of gender, that weigh in excess of 75 pounds are wild boar and are usually claimed to be Russian or razorback regardless of sex or genetic background in an ever-expanding clutter of frenzied feral hog interbreeding of widespread geographic proportions.

In a way pig stories sort of parallel those about black bears. Hardly anyone has ever shot a black bear that weighed less than 200 pounds. I have seen a ton of pictures of pointy-nosed, pixie-eared deceased black bear (I have a couple of my own) neatly captioned: "Me and my 200-pound bear." Not 165, 196 or 211 pounds—200! Likewise, nearly every picture anyone has ever shown me of a cannily collected wild pig showcased a "wild boar."

When I was a kid and everything was romantically newborn fresh, the notion of bowhunting wild boar was looked upon as a seriously dangerous proposition. I can recall conversations in which gun-toting fellows of my early acquaintance flatly stated that it couldn't be done. There was this bullet-resistant armor-plate fable to begin with, a notion that the hide covering a wild boar's vitals was impervious to anything less than a creation of Roy Weatherby. They claimed hide so stout it "would bend any little ol' arra"! Tales of the tank-like constitution of wild hogs were punctuated with accounts of how so and so had made it to a convenient tree, just barely....

I can also recall the skull of a substantial wild pig that Howard Hill once showed me. Perfectly grouped in its center was a pair of his trademark three-to-one-ratio slender broadheads, placed there when the pig—this one a boar with legitimate tusks—had had the audacity to charge. Well, I thought then, and still do, that if anyone could pull off that sort of touch-and-go shooting, it was Howard.

There has always been something fascinating about hunting wild hogs...er, I mean boar. You see, everyone goes hunting for wild boar.

Of course, I heard all of the stories then, and still do today—fearsome tales, some of them, mostly campfire bourbon talk. However, there are those that are based on some grisly facts.

Tales of the dangers of bowhunting wild boar are common.

Short of sallying off to darkest Africa, where there are some things that can stomp, toss or bite you in half, or an ill-fated, statistically improbable bad-luck encounter with a bad North American bear, there's really not much around here capable of separating you from any of your precious parts except an encounter with the wrong pig at the wrong time.

This has been known to happen.

Good wild boar, that is to say mature males, can possess teeth of significant size—nasty things that they continuously hone one upon the other to a keenness that rivals any broadhead.

Let's get into some biology here. Boars are male pigs. Female pigs are sows. Young pigs are piglets or shoats (whatever that means), and all of the above, when harvested by a hunter, are wild boar, the hunting of which frequently causes more anxiety than a call from the IRS.

There is some merit in being concerned, which brings us back to the matter of teeth.

Grown-up boy pigs, usually those over 100 pounds or so—it depends a lot upon genetics—start to feel pretty pugnacious when their sabers begin protruding from their lips. They fight a great deal among themselves and don't seem to care much for anything except their own well-being.

Mayhem, when it comes to hunting pig—uh, I mean boar—most commonly takes place when the outing is tailored around the use of dogs. As a friend of mine puts it: "Statistically, it's like the morning freeways in Los Angeles. Eventually, there will be a wreck!" Let me point out that the hunting of pigs with dogs is a common and accepted practice and quite practical in many areas that wild pigs inhabit due to the impenetrable haunts they prefer and a strong reluctance to leave them other than under the cover of night. And again I should mention that a mature pig (boar or sow) is a savvy customer, quite intelligent, set in its ways and commonly short-fused.

I was once party to the collection of a pig (the owner of the dogs called him a "hawg," which means the same thing) that carried credentials equal to any fabled whitetail you may have heard of. Lord only knows how many leathernecked dogs he sent to the Final Kennel. His tally sheet included a hamstrung horse and many of those "he made it to the tree just barely" tales. The hog's notoriety had grown over a five or six-year period, which would have made him twice that age when a friend of mine shot him. He filled the bed of a '76 model Chevy half-ton pickup with the tailgate down and tipped some honest scales at 513 pounds—dressed! He came out on the losing side that day, though he mauled two dogs in the process, and made a grand pile of sausage.

Early archers shot wild pigs from horsedrawn chariots and from astride galloping steeds, while others, depicted in art, stalked and shot them afoot, as most of us do today. It seems that for the thousands of years that man has held to the bow, wild hogs have been accorded prime respect, the boar equal to the stag. I believe that it had to do with the teeth.

I was thinking about that when I last hunted wild pigs with my close friend George Wright. It was in one of his secret places where he has taken scores. A very good pig was coming toward us.

"When we shoot him, we'll jump up and charge. Make a lot of noise."

"Huh?"

"Yeah, the best defense is a good offense."

"You read that somewhere, right, Wright?"

"No, that's what I do."

"What happens if it doesn't work?"

"See that tree?"

"Yeah."

"Go for it."

"That's not much of a tree!"

"You probably won't have to."

"Super!"   ▲

Small Guests That Bite

Before us stood a wall of that impenetrable brush South Texas is famous for. Six- to 10-feet tall, it crowded the wandering sendero carved years past by the labored churning of some bladed mechanical monster. Nothing less could have shaped a road in that brush.

The morning was windless, with just enough of a chill to make the magnesium handle riser unpleasant to hold. So, I slipped a soft-leather batting glove on my bow hand, and I looked for the right spot to set up. The new day's sun at our backs cut orange creases through the tangled web of brush before us. The sun was rising with incredible pace; you could almost feel the planet turning. The shadows would soon be gone.

Behind us on the sendero lay the still steaming sign of a passing band of javelina. Up awfully early, I thought when we cut it. My partner scrunched himself in the tattered snag of a ruined, run-over mesquite; I settled on my knees in waist-high grass 20 yards to his right. The rising sun brought on a slight crossing breeze that was just perfect.

With full camo and face masks in place, we became indistinguishable—just a couple more mottled bumps in a cleared place full of lumps and bumps. I laid the trim Hoyt Spectra loaded with an XX75 before me while slipping the lanyard with its set of calls from inside my jacket. I could barely see my partner, but I knew his bow would be in hand, arrow nocked and ready to draw. We were both pretty sure about what was going to happen. I put the Jones call to my lips and cut loose.

It's been over 35 years since I called my first javelina. It was rather by accident. I was trying to lure a coyote at the time, and a single old boar came boiling in instead. He was safe from a legal point of view—the season was open, I think, but I didn't have a license. Thirty-five years ago the little pigs had the hyped reputation for meanness—ornery critters that would tear apart man or beast. Fiction to be sure, though we weren't all too sure then. He rattled me some, that old boar did. At the time I wasn't sure how things were going to turn out. Well, as you have gathered, he didn't eat me. No, as a matter of fact, he ran off in a panic when I jumped in his face.

Naturally, the episode got me thinking, and campfire discussions with many of my Arizona varmint-calling companeros revealed that more than one javelina had blundered into coyote-calling setups. Sometimes they showed up in woofing, tooth-popping gangs. For a bunch of eager young bowhunters, it was an intriguing possibility to set about exploring.

The first time I purposely called javelina—when it actually worked—was spectacular. It was a beautiful late morning during Arizona's January archery javelina season. I had glassed and tromped a lot of javelinaless miles and was circling back toward camp when I topped a slight ridge above an arroyo. Below me a quarter mile, I spotted something out of place and sat down to put the binocular to work. The grassy edge of the arroyo was alive with pigs.

By now I had learned about the importance of a favorable wind, and that calling from a position above the pigs was far better than any other. Both conditions were luckily in my favor. It wasn't difficult to get within 100 yards to a place that offered a good natural blind setup. From there I could see many of the "javies" feeding, and one old boar who was intent on procreating looked to be the biggest javelina in Arizona.

I got locked and loaded, situated myself comfortably and cut a barrage loose with the loudest call in my arsenal, my favorite contest call. It instantly became my favorite javelina call. Every pig in the bunch—there must have been at least 30—were up and coming at me in a heartbeat. It was almost scary. They closed with unbelievable speed, milling, woofing, bristling fiercely. I was overrun: Trying to shoot and call fragmented my composure. They ran off, I called them back; they ran off, I called them back again. Finally, I got one with my fifth arrow. I was glad. I only had six to begin with, and the remaining one was a blunt!

Because some of you will be interested in calling javelina, I will now impart my secret technique. This is precious stuff gathered over countless encounters and the participation of hundreds upon hundreds of javelina. I do not share it with just anyone; knowledge gained over decades of field research passed on unselfishly should deserve respect. Pay close attention.

Avail yourself of a varmint call (or javelina call, as they are basically the same thing) designated as a Long Range or jackrabbit-voiced call. These are loud calls, and loud is important. At the chosen calling site, hyperventilate to fill your lungs with as much air as possible. Then proceed to place all that air into the call in loud, screeching wails of stark, terror-ridden pandemonium. Do not cease. If javelina appear, keep it up; blow it right in their face. Keep it up until you have shot a javelina, run out of arrows or collapsed from exhaustion. There are no subtleties, no cute tricks, no special techniques. Hard and loud is it.

There. Now you know.

So, what happened on that clean South Texas morning? I was grinning to myself in anticipation of the impending action. This is going to be too good!

The harsh screeching of the first series of calls had barely cut the air when the brush churned close by—much closer than I thought they were. The air was instantly laden with the thick, wild scent of excited javelina: feet stomped, brush crackled, teeth clattered, pigs woofed and grunted in anxious confusion. I was calling one-handed now—the loaded Spectra up and pointed. The woofing faded, as did the sound of tiny, split-toed feet. Their aroma hung heavy with the silence.

Sometimes calling javelina doesn't work at all.　　　Ⱥ

Gobbler Intelligence Tests

I t has taken better than a quarter of my lifetime to reach a conclusion that seriously contradicts most popular opinion. Revelations of this magnitude should not be taken lightly.

There is, however, a certain selfishness in all of us about revealing the truth, truths that are not easily recognized or obtained, which provide inside edges not easy to part with. I have wrestled with the dilemma and reached the proper decision. The world is entitled to the truth: Turkeys are not smart.

From the Piney Woods of Alabama to the badlands of the Dakotas, from the mesquite flats of Texas to the blue ridgetops of the Ozarks, cries of heresy, boos, taunts and barbs will doubtless follow.

A mature gobbler can stand some three-feet tall, and on occasion can weigh in excess of 30 pounds. He can make his head, which is about the size of your fist, turn all the colors of the American flag one at a time or collectively. He was born (hatched actually) schizo—suspicious, paranoid and remains that way throughout life. His eyesight surpasses phenomenal by a factor of 10, though he does not (thank God!) have a measurable capacity for smell. He is undeniably magnificent in a strange, different sort of way. He eludes pursuers by the hundreds, and this has established a legendary status shaped amidst the smoke of thousands of springtime campfires.

He is all of these, but he ain't smart.

In my life I have met a dozen or so turkeys that, at the onset (before my great revelation), I accorded the capacity for thought. I have sat with companions who in the glow of dying coals gave mental credentials to certain birds that would rival a bus load of Rhodes scholars. And, I confess, I too supported such reasoning for sometime. It is important during the Spring Ritual that such birds be honored with names. The Racehorse (I hated him!), Stumpy, Sod Creek Runner, Ol' Double G and Round Top Willy come to mind. They became our legends, our obsessions; we loved and hated them.

The truth, however, was not that they were beating us up by virtue of their alleged advanced IQs. In retrospect we beat ourselves with incautious, overeager, impatient pursuit, all part of the never-ending learning curve. Such old birds are cautious and contrary providing free passes to major migraines, just cause for switching from steel tips to copper-plated sixes. Even then, it is seldom a level field of play.

I love tough, old, long-spurred turkeys. I am no longer intimidated by them. I have come to realize that they are tough because the are cautious, suspicious paranoids. I have established that their brain is smaller than mine, therefore my capacity to outmaneuver them mentally is greater. I have also recognized that a great deal of their success in avoiding any fatal contact is most often simply a matter of luck. I know that if I am persistent enough, careful enough, and patient enough to sit as still as the stump I'm camouflaged to resemble, that eventually they will run out of luck.

In fact, if I may be allowed to throw a little fat on the fire, they can be downright stupid.

Last season, a good friend with whom I share some secret

turkey spots was giving me regular evening reports on the battle he was engaged in with a double-bearded monster in southeastern Missouri. This man is truly an expert turkey hunter possessed of a fanatical need to hunt turkeys in no less than five states for no less than six straight weeks, minimum! His duel with the double-bearded bronze monster had played his patience to a dangerously thin edge. The migraine syndrome was upon him, primarily I thought, as he recited the day's events, because he wanted to get that turkey killed and get on to South Dakota. Well, the bird's string of luck had held, hairline close twice, but it held. You have heard a hundred similar stories. He'd almost come, he'd hang up, he'd strut in full view for 20 minutes and walk off gobbling his brains out. Once he came in silently, from behind, spooked and flew to the next mountain. He was always alone; strangely, no hens cluttered the stage. But that's how it was. Then his luck ran out at 10:45 a.m. on the last day my friend had to hunt. How? Let's see.

The Bronze Baron (he had a name by now) sounded off twice on the roost at daylight and never made another peep all morning. Defeated, my friend came to an old wooden gate at the base of the hardwood ridge that grated open with the strident screech of a startled housecat when he opened it. The Baron double-gobbled from 100 yards away. Wiggle the gate, screech again. With a whopping, flopping of wings the bird pitched off the ridge and sailed into a running landing headed straight for the gate. His pendulum beards swayed from side to side, and he was gobbling his head off. At eight steps the Baron's lucky streak came to an abrupt stop. Smart turkey? Killed by a gate!

I rest my case.

Chapter 7

Mailbag

Questions From All Over

Being accorded the privilege of authoring this page some half dozen or so issues ago was a pleasure. Since then, I have received a variety of correspondence that has contained both interesting remarks and questions—even the occasional accolade—from a widespread scattering of our country's archery hunters. A handful of letters has been mixed in from far and wide, even from folks overseas who share a mutual affinity for bows and arrows. It has really been interesting. I have been advised on occasion (never face to face) that my perspectives on bowhunting—what it's about, how I choose to do it, my opinions on equipment or the fact that I have never shot a Pope & Young whitetail—categorize me as something somewhere between an incompetent and a nerd. I confess to being unlucky rather than incompetent in the matter of a Pope & Young whitetail. My latest victory in that category netted 124 inches dead-solid even, exactly three-fourths of an inch less than my best ever. Think about that one for a second!

Anyhow, without necessarily quoting verbatim, let me walk

you through a smattering of the comments and questions that I have received over the past year. Admittedly, these have been cherry-picked from files that I have chosen to keep, which obviously eliminates the dweebs!

You knew and hunted with Fred Bear. Was he the best bowhunter?

To my mind he was the greatest bowhunter, not necessarily the best. I think there's very rarely any such thing as the "best" in hunting, be it bowhunter, duck or deer hunter for that matter (although I knew an Arizona man once, Sam Dudley, who was considered by all who had the pleasure of knowing him as being the best varmint-calling coyote hunter of all time.) That's a serious assessment, and he deserved it. Fred Bear was a superb woodsman, a keen naturalist and a compassionate hunter. He was and is acclaimed as being the father of modern bowhunting, a mantle he wore with quiet dignity. There will never be another like him—not even close. Considering that, he was as close to the best as you can get.

Looking back through all my old (emphasis on old) magazines, I see you shot a recurve for years. Did you quit because a compound is better?

While I'm not over the hill, the crest is in clear view. Aging bone and sinew egg on creaking joints to an ever-increasing symphony of snaps and pops. Too many years of too-heavy bows haven't helped. When shooting, my body begins to sound like a pan of Jiffy Pop in the microwave. This is all compounded (excuse me) by my tendency to have become lazier in midlife. Shooting a recurve well takes a greater commitment to practice. I chose an alternative because it wasn't worth the physical aggravation. I saw no reason to continue the abuse, and, in fact, was told by doctors that I should actually quit. Fat chance! I can shoot a compound extremely well, with considerably less stay-in-tune time. That's important to me, and no, they are not better tools in my opinion, just a bit easier. Mulling it over in my mind, I believe that some of the finest, most consistently successful bowhunters I know today still favor a recurve.

The following was a recent letter from a friend in Arizona who gloated: *Well, we sure kicked their butts on Prop 200!*

Oh, really! Sixty-two to 38 simply tells me that almost 40-percent of the population thought it was a splendid idea. Talk about nerds and dweebs! Winning by 13-percent is certainly a pure victory, but hardly a thrashing. Heck, there was one county where the vote was an even split. This took place in Arizona, the Wild West where folks still bust bulls, ride broncs and drive around with carbines in their pick'em-up trucks. This is a state with tons of huntable public lands; though, for sure, it is a state that is being crushed under the population expansion. This scares me.

You know something else that both scares and irks me? To the best of my knowledge, the only industry that dove right in and ponied up the bucks—major big bucks—in the most important anti-hunting issue we have ever faced was the archery industry: AMO, the Archery Manufacturers Organization, along with many independent bowhunting organizations. Other equally threatened industries and other "hunting organizations" were either uninvolved or chose to go a separate, ununited way. I'm proud of the archery industry and am reminded that we have more than our share of those dreaded nerds within our (all hunters') ranks. This reminds me, there are a couple of organizations that won't see any more of my membership bucks. I'll just raise the ante for the WLFA's Bowhunter Defense Coalition. You should too.

I have learned that in your country the javelina is good not to eat and is also more dangerous. You are most brave hunting them. I will hunt them too in your state of Texas in the next year. Will they attack us?

Ahh, it's fine to be considered a big, bad, brave archery hunter. The writer, along with two friends, are young Japanese archers with no place in their country to hunt and heads full of exciting visions. The lure of some potential danger pulled them though. They were obviously filled with some trepidation and quite concerned about hunting something that they could not eat. It was fun to steer them in the direction of a friend with some serious Texas property and a passel of "good not to eat" javies. Having experienced enough real Japanese food, I found it difficult to imagine their concern about eating anything. Certainly, javelina have to be as good as a plateful of fugu, that poisonous fish they lust for at megabucks a bite. Anyway, I spoke to Yoshi on the phone when the archers arrived at Houston Intercontinental. I told him it was best to attack from out of the sun. He thought that was excellent advice, his grandfather having been a fighter pilot! They are down there right now. I hope to meet up with them before they leave.

You have the dumbest, stupidest opinions of broadheads of anyone I've ever read!

Whoops, a dweeb. Is he right? It's a possibility.

I have read and admired you for years. When are you going to get that Pope & Young whitetail? I sure hope you do.

It will happen this year, on the 13th of November at exactly 9:52 a.m. He was pre-scouted, but that went up in smoke as soon as the rut started, so I strategically moved into his hot rut pattern and stimulated him with a mixture of exotic pheromones, some rattling and a super-cool blend of tending buck grunts. I got a 23-yard quartering-away angled shot from a stand nine feet high that afforded the absolute dead-solid perfect-impact area. He was 6½ years old, field-dressed at 187 pounds (a bit rundown, no fat!) and netted 167³/₈ inches typical points. You can wake me now!   ▲

Dear
Jim

Most letters I receive are addressed Dear Jim or Dear Mr. Dougherty, yet one fellow wrote three times to Jimbo. I guess that means we're buddies, and I suspect we are.

While some letters are simply complimentary, which honestly does give me a warm, cozy feeling, most pose a question or seek my advice or opinion. Occasionally—not often—someone will take me to task. That's become rarer, though, and hasn't happened in the last year or so, which makes me wonder if I'm doing something wrong.

Frequently, the letters end with an invitation to join the writer on a hunt. These invitations invariably are mildly apologetic: I can't promise you a really big buck, but we have some nice ones around here. Gads, do I want to go to a place where someone can promise me a really big buck? Once last year a lovely female bowhunter tendered an invitation to hunt the Ohio farm she acquired in her recent divorce. The enclosed photograph of a fine buck included herself. My wife said I could not go.

Actually, I don't want to go someplace where I'm promised a really big buck, or anything else for that matter. What's the point? The joy is in the anticipation, speculation and challenge. Going someplace with the potential of big bucks or big bulls is different; we all want to go to those places.

Surprisingly, most of the letters I received over the last year, ones that sought some hunting advice, did not deal with whitetails. Maybe that's not so surprising. Certainly word on my big-buck ineptitude has circulated.

There were some whitetail queries last year, to be sure, but the letters covered a variety of topics. Here are some excerpts:

Do you hunt whitetails by the moon? Only when it's up during the day. Otherwise, I hunt during legal shooting hours.

Do you think that bigger antlers are better for rattling than smaller sets? Yes, but smaller sets are easier to carry and don't mash your fingers as bad.

Is the rutting season the best time to kill a really big buck, and what state would you pick? How would I know, I've never killed a really big buck. Statistically, the answer is yes, during midday, incidentally. However, I think early-season bucks can be very predictable, therefore very vulnerable, while still on their late-summer pre-rut patterns. State-wise, I would pick Iowa or Kansas.

Do I have to shoot a record-book whitetail to become a member of the Pope & Young Club? No. Anyone who has taken an adult North American big game animal (it doesn't have to be record class, and it can be of either sex) can join the club as an associate member. Regular membership is achieved by associate tenure and the criteria of three species, one of which has to be record class.

What's your favorite grunt call? One that a buck responds to. Seriously, I'm partial to the Lohman Model 40 Mega Grunt.

I have read that you prefer bright fletching on your arrows. Won't bright fletching give you away and spook deer and elk? I use bright fletching (chartreuse Trueflight feathers) so I can see where my arrows go. This way I can find them easier after I miss. I also prefer bright, fluorescent green Easton 3-D Super Nocks for the same reason. I want to see the arrow impact point as clearly as possible. Under low light, this combination gives me great in-flight visibility. Yes, bright fletching could give you away with too much movement so you have to be careful. I think the value of bright fletching outweighs the risk. I'm very careful and can't remember when I last thought my fletching gave me away. Of course, there are camo covers available for hiding bright fletching.

I met you at the Ohio Deer Classic and you talked a bit about elk hunting. I want to try it this year. Should I learn to call? Should I book with a guide? Would you use an expandable head? I certainly recommend that first-time elk hunters make arrangements with an outfitter. This is especially important if you're not experienced with mountain-style hunting and its varied conditions. It's different and difficult. If you go with an outfitter, all you have to do is hunt, eat and sleep. It maximizes your available time. Get references from any outfitter you contact and talk with them rather than write. Ask pertinent questions about equipment, staff, food and accommodations. Ask them if they would go back.

The outfitter's guides will do the calling. Look at your first elk hunt as an enjoyable learning experience. Until you have some experience calling, they would much rather you kept quiet and did what you're told. If you book a hunt, be sure to advise the outfitter of your physical condition and any dietary or medical problems. Can he handle those? Get in the best shape you possibly can, even easy elk hunts are pretty tough. Do it, there's nothing like it. And no, I would not use an expandable head.

You must feel pretty fortunate to have been able to bowhunt so much in so many places. How does your wife put up with your being gone so much? This part, incidentally, was an addendum to a letter by a young lady. Yes, I have been very, very lucky, and yes, I am gone quite a bit from September through January. Then comes spring turkey season, but that's only five weeks or so. So, how does my wife (of nearly 40 years, by the way) feel about it? There was a time once, when she said, tongue in cheek, "Leave you! How do you leave someone who's not there?" She doesn't put up with it; she wants to be there when I come back. I look forward to getting back. Like I said, I've been very, very lucky.

I'm going to buy a new hunting bow this year. What's your opinion on the one-cam configuration? I started shooting one late last season (Hoyt Stratus Carbonite) and love it. I cannot believe how quiet it is—a feature I feel is very important—and, of course, it is literally maintenance free, nothing goes out of whack. Four whitetails and two coyotes never heard it go off. I'm sticking with it!

Offering opinions, suggestions or advice if I feel qualified is but one side of a two-way street. The best side is when you are on the receiving end, when something of value comes your way.   ▲

Personal Preferences

One of the things guys in my line of work—those who have been involved with archery, bowhunting and the outdoor industry for years who write, speak, sit on manufacturer's advisory staffs and enjoy a certain degree of celebrity—do is field a lot of questions.

One thing I should mention is that guys (and gals, too) in my line of work, though they are generally friendly and respectful of one another—and frequent hunting companions—do not necessarily agree on matters of equipment or hunting technique.

The best thing about this diversity is it gives folks options to ponder, or perhaps on occasion a revelation that might solve someone's problem. Personally, especially in a hunting camp environment, I enjoy sharing perspectives and preferences with fellow hunters when we warm up on the practice butt, organize our gear or sip something around the fire. In the last few months in two camps in Colorado and another in far northern Quebec, I shared hard hunting days and relaxing good times with a grand assortment of people and came home to a desk piled with mail.

One of the letter-writers inquired about peep sights. (He noted in photos it appears I don't use one.) That, upon reflection, is one of the most frequent inquiries I run into at camps when someone takes a look at my equipment. Well, I don't use one! If I did, there's no doubt I could shoot tighter groups. I shot recurves bare bow (instinctively) for nearly 30 years by looking through the string and shot compounds the same way when I crossed over. I still do that today with a sight. Unless they are substantially reamed out, peeps are tough to see through in poor light; and aiming around them is a bad, often disastrous, poor deal. I shoot pretty good target groups as it is—good, not nock-splitting great—though I did Robin Hood two arrows last spring. My bowhunting groups require only one arrow. I don't use a stabilizer either, though one would help with tighter groups, too. They do reduce noise and torque, but my bow's very quiet; and I like mine as lightweight as possible. If I was interested in competition I'd use both. But I'm not.

Ah, bow speed, the omnipresent topic. A fellow in one camp announced emphatically that you cannot tune a bow to shoot broadheads at speeds in excess of 260 fps and that mechanical heads are the only solution. Well, golly gee whiz, I never knew that! My new bow shoots exactly 260 fps, which incidentally is the fastest bow I ever used. Most have been in the 230-240 fps range, and I've been able to tune them to shoot a shovel. But this new Hoyt turned out to be pretty damn trouble-free and quick, and shoots Thunderhead 100s like a dream. I must have misunderstood; maybe he said 261!

A nice fellow from Michigan asked me a fair question: "You're an Easton Guy, right?" "You bet!" I replied. "How come you're not shooting A/C/Cs?" We kicked that around for a while, him thinking it was a step up that would provide more accuracy and speed, me responding with the fact that I didn't see a need or advantage. Hell's bells, I don't shoot well enough to enjoy all the accuracy inherent in an XX78! Changing over to the properly spined carbon composite would give me all of another seven or eight feet per second. I like enough shaft diameter for five-inch feather-fletched stability; maybe that's why my broadheads tune well at 260!

I like feathers. I think they steer a little better, but that may just be an old-fashioned quirk in my mind. However, I do believe they're more forgiving coming off or through a rest. I also like simple arrow rests without prongs, springs or nuts and bolts. I use a N.A.P. Centerest. When it wears down—once a year if I shoot a lot—I just stick another shelf cap in place. Nothing changes. I've read you can't hardly shoot this sort of rest with a short bow and release, but then I've read a lot of strange things. I suppose in some respects I'm a dinosaur, equipment-wise; Heaven knows I'm not into a lot of bells and whistles.

A fellow in Canada was concerned and asked me why I carried only four arrows. As he put it, "I lacked firepower," and I suspect he figured I was show-boating when I showed him one was a Judo. Well, certainly there was a chance I'd run out, though the third could easily be converted. Firepower's for wars. If I miss four shots—and I have—it's time to head back to camp for a nap. I love bow quivers, and I'm certainly not a good enough archer to notice any point of impact change as their load is reduced, as I've read. However, they will move a bow arm around in the wind when hunting open country, so I suspect carrying two would be better; but I don't think I need that much sleep.

Archery equipment is neat. Don't be misled by my attitude to think that I don't play around and shoot most of it enough to understand how it works. The equipment and the questions we all get about it are fun and let us express our point of view. Admittedly, mine favors some simplicity; this doesn't make it absolute—just mine. But you know what I do believe is absolute? I believe our equipment is just a fraction of the bowhunting experience, that shooting it is just the last piece in the exciting puzzle that gets us there. There's a theme today that suggests equipment makes the bowhunter. That's not true. Only bowhunting makes a bowhunter.

Chapter 8

Exceptional Animals

Remembering
Monster Mulies

"Tell me about bowhunting mule deer in the old days. You old-timers must have seen some sights." Framing the young editor in the V created by my crossed, elevated feet was like putting him comfortably at the bottom notch of an old buckhorn sight.

The editor was a pup in the '60s, if indeed he was even born then. It would be nice if he could have seen the West when it was literally teeming with big mule deer, when private ranchland was often available for the asking, before the garbage from too many slobs locked the gates and raised the ante. Back then, prime public land was really ours to use, uncluttered by too many cattle, political pressure and more garbage.

There are still plenty of mule deer. They have not vanished, nor are they endangered, though the numbers have certainly declined from the golden days of two to three decades ago when herds of big bucks were a commonplace. Of course, there are still places here and there with good herds of really big deer, mostly private land that anyone can hunt if their pockets are deep enough. There are also public areas managed for trophy deer with limited permits on the draw.

Stretching myself into a sitting position, I removed the editor's mug from my make-believe sight to face him full on and tell him about the Kaibab Plateau in the '60s. It was nothing to see 200 to 300 deer feeding in the meadows along Highway 67 from Jacobs Lake to the Kaibab Lodge, a trip of perhaps 20 miles. Many of them were huge bucks. It was the optimum adrenaline rush.

Although the meadows were off-limits, the surrounding forest held many thousands of acres loaded with deer. We would drive the criss-crossing labyrinth of logging roads, searching for deer concentrations. We would eventually find an area stiff with deer. Within a mile or two we might see 30 to 50 mule deer. Half of them would be bucks. Some of them were bruisers; bucks that looked so big they were kind of scary. Usually these concentrations were in fresh logging areas where quaking aspen slash littered the ground. Sometimes the deer revolved around an explosion of mushrooms. The deer concentrations were food-oriented. That was the first place we really began to understand one of deer hunting's basic elements: find the food, there are the deer.

The Kaibab was a fabulous place to see deer and that alone attracted a lot of bowhunters, but the mature pine forest was really rather tough to hunt. We didn't know anything about tree stands then. They sure would have worked. Our tactics and techniques were just being learned. Mainly we just sort of snuck around, and we learned how to do that fairly well. Some truly big deer were taken, though not as many as you might expect, considering how many monsters were running about.

Bowhunters got quite a few average deer, though. Big bucks have never been easy even when there are lots of them. Maybe our equipment had something to do with it. You see, hardly anyone back in those days would dream of shooting farther than 40 yards, maybe not even that. The open country worked against us. It was fairly easy to get within 60 yards, but that was still too far. I suppose with today's equipment it could be different if we could find the same opportunities.

You would have loved Nevada, I told the editor, especially the Jarbridge Club. It was a meeting-place bar in little more than a mining ghost town crowded in the evenings with the bowhunting legends of the time.

Jarbridge is in extreme northeastern Nevada, maybe 10 miles from the Idaho border. You got there on one of the nastiest roads in the world. I don't know who discovered and started the annual September migration, but the word was out, and bowmen with dreams of big bucks came from everywhere. At the rear of the bar there was a solid pine panel filled with the arrows of successful bowmen. Ray Torrey had a group in the lower right-hand corner you couldn't get your fingers around. You shot in your arrow and circled it with your name. I got to stick one in there, too; up there with guys like Jack Howard, Hugh Rick, Frank Boscarino, George Kili, and Bill Otto. The club hummed with a happy, relaxed atmosphere, as did the deer camps around the quaint old Western town. Everyone was there to have a good time. They did, and they took a lot of big deer, too.

Nevada was unreal in the '60s. One evening I counted 37 mature four-point mulies together in one sage and aspen basin. In the tall sage, their brown velvet antlers swayed like the waving legs of huge inverted tarantulas. Everything was going along just swell...'til the wind switched. That's when I started to learn about how thermal reversals would eat your lunch. That hasn't changed.

On one late-afternoon deer drive through a patch above Foreman Creek (probably no more than two acres in size) 14 bucks blew out in every direction. Most of them were "bookers" for sure. No one touched a hair. It was good spot-and-stalk country with plenty of cover and little out-of-the-way niches and pockets that held big bucks you could work. Guys like Torrey and Kili would backpack into those places. I remember when Kili hauled out a buck with a 32-inch spread. The local cowboys hardly gave it a glance. In those days a 32-inch deer wouldn't even be in the running for greatest spread at the big deer contests in Las Vegas and Reno. We always stopped there to sign up on our way to Arizona, Nevada or Utah.

It was the same for big bucks around Wells to the east of Elko in the Humboldt Range. South and east, down around Pioche, closer to the Utah border was different but ideal for bowhunting. We never had any trouble finding lots of deer then; big deer in Nevada, Utah, Arizona or Colorado. We were really just learning. Man, it would have been nice to know then what we do now!

In Colorado, it was not at all unusual to see a dozen bucks a day that would score in the 180s. That was before the shale oil exploration boom began probing everywhere. Mule deer don't do nearly as well around man as whitetails. They are more vulnerable to his pressures. I guess history has proven that. Once the big bucks are knocked back and the pressure maintained for several seasons, not many get a chance to grow to potential. It's tough for a deer to last five or six seasons today except on controlled land.

The editor's eyes were lost in thought. Their glaze had ebbed a bit, though they still sparkled with the vision of a dozen gray-muzzled old bucks with rocking-chair racks feeding in a faraway sage pocket he might find for himself.

"Sad, isn't it?" he said. "Getting a record-class mulie today is one of the hardest things to do."

"It's probably the hardest," I replied. "But it always has been. Buy us another round, and I'll tell you about a couple of places I know."   ▲

Versus
Ursus

Bear hunting is a fascinating, often addicting, pastime for many, though I've never felt any compelling urge to collect all the species. After my first one (the second honestly—the first one wasn't really very big), I've looked on the subject of bears rather passively, being an antlers and horns guy at heart. I have many good friends, though, solid, serious, hardcore archery hunters, who drool at the prospect of bowhunting bruins. I admire, but do not share their enthusiasm.

It's not that I don't respect bears (I do), nor do I have any anthropomorphic cartoon-oriented huggy bear ideology. Neither am I scared of them, though several have given me cause. I have done enough bear hunting, black bears mostly, to achieve reasonable success. I've hunted with hounds, over bait, and even stalked a few. The last one I shot I called up with a varmint call. I made a lackadaisical run in the brown bear department once, too. A brownie, or Kodiak, is a pretty formidable beast. All we ran across were immature juveniles not worth troubling over according to my companion, though they looked bigger than all get out to me.

Once, years ago, when adventurous bear hunters such as Ken Oldham and Eddie King flew out of Kotzebue, Alaska, and the white infinity of our polar ice fields was still open to polar bear hunting, I turned down an invitation from Eddie to make a run at one of those great creatures. It was an opportunity as good as any archery hunter will ever get, and it was free! The passage of time has given me frequent cause to question that decision.

I can recall clearly Eddie's invitation (I don't remember the exact year, late '60s sometime), when my secretary indicated she had a "funny-sounding phone call". King was on a static, garbled radiophone trying, with some difficulty, to tell me about a dead whale on the ice drawing a constant stream of hungry bears.

He was really fired up. It was the best bowhunting setup for a polar bear he had ever run across, and all I had to do was get there. Well, I had to do the protocol thing and pass it by the higher-up powers in my life. The higher-ups said, "Sure." I thought they would. The perceived promotional value was certainly worth the price of air fare to Kotzebue. We were selling a lot of Pearson Mercury Marauders back then. Supporting the sales effort with in-the-field research was the highlight of my job description. Anyhow, when King radio-phoned the following day, I simply wasn't all that interested.

Time, of course, allows you to reflect on the folly of your ways. Deep inside I do not regret the fact that I didn't try for a polar bear. What I regret is not having seen the gnarly, frostbitten face of the ice pack, knowing now that I probably never will. I should have grabbed the experience.

Bears conjure up some wild emotions among men, inherent, no doubt, from days long past when bears ate more men than men ate bears. It used to come with the territory.

Some of my bear hunting has been camps designed solely for that purpose. In several instances, I have seen grown men with above-average hunting experience wilt completely under the pressure of dealing with a black bear from a tree stand over bait.

Now, let's be honest about it. There is something deep-wrenching, viscerally scary about bears to many people. Even a really nice, average black bear weighing less than 200 pounds will, when very close, chill a hunter to the bone. Some get turned on by it, others crash.

This sense of bear dread is not unusual. I know several people who severely suffer from it. There's no disgrace in it. "Scared of bear" themes are a regular thread in the tales of many bear hunting outfitters' fireside stories. Perhaps they're designed to steel the spirit of the unannointed, but, having heard a few, I've been struck with the notion that it was simply too much corn mash talking in a counterproductive direction. Fear of bears is not uncommon, nor for that matter is the fool-ishness of some I've met who treat them without proper caution.

The squared rug of a really fine black bear graces one of our office walls. It's a chocolate-brown-phase blackie that genuinely weighed 400 pounds and change. It commonly inspires more awe than my Cape buffalo from Africa, which is considered to be infinitely more dangerous. Visitors to our offices, especially non-outdoor types, consider the bear scary, while the buffalo's black, belligerent bulk seems far less intimidating with its rather bovine look. I might mention that the bear came a lot closer to getting a piece of me than the Cape buffalo.

This bear was a big old bugger, fat from a plentiful summer, and with a size 16 track. Our pack of tested bear dogs was made up of fierce fellows with a thick logbook of bears under its belt. They didn't intimidate him in the slightest. Going up a tree wasn't in his game plan; he liked to fight on the ground. It took all day to catch up with him, a day of the sort I hope never to repeat.

It was hot, dry, inhospitable country of one steep canyon after another. This was an animal whose nerves were as worn and frazzled from the day-long battle with the hounds as ours were in the pursuit. When we finally caught up with that bear, I shot him. He pinpointed this latest aggravation with furious intent, zeroed in on my belt buckle and came at me with the heart-stopping momentum of a train. Only when you have seen it first hand can the speed of a bear register properly on a mind warped by ponderous cartoon impressions. Only the intervention of a stout-hearted hound, already fearfully shredded by whipping claws, deflected the bear's intent to decimate us. He provided the precious time I needed to place a final broadhead.

When the battle ended in the boulders and brambles of that shadowy, bottomless canyon, with the echoes of barking and yelling fading into the sunset, the dry, croaky-soft voice of Ed Vance (who held his tattered, big-hearted dog) uttered, "Mercy, me. That was too dang close!"

I have seen the accounting of enough bears to reach double-digit figures. That's certainly no record, but it does establish a base. On five occasions now I have seen a black bear show its front side with fierce, back-bowed tooth-chomping determination. My point is that black bears shouldn't be taken as lightly as seems commonplace.

I suppose you can go through a lifetime of shooting black bears like they were so many cottontail rabbits, giving the endeavor only a cursory three on the 10-scale of adrenaline rushes. I have friends who look at bear hunting as little more than a small-game romp. But, having seen my share of black bears that vigorously tried to take on some seriously armed hunters, I'm thinking it's on a higher plane than a cottontail hunt. I suppose it's because I've never seen a cottontail rabbit charge.   ♠

Really Big Deer

I n the ebbing glow of a pink-hued Alberta sunset, he was the biggest whitetail buck I have ever seen. Over the years I have seen a few truly big whitetails, and like most hunters, I've seen many others that, at the time and in the clutches of an adrenaline attack, appeared to be truly huge but weren't. Shooters, yes, but not really huge.

I think I know what a monstrous, really big, butt-kicking buck looks like. Over the last 20 years or so, I have actually held most of the biggest bow-killed whitetail bucks in my hands, measured them at Pope & Young panels, hefted their weight, marveled at the outlandish girth of base and main beams and caressed the smooth length of perfect points.

Sometimes it makes you want to scream, "Why can't I have one?"

East of Edmonton, Alberta, angling somewhat south across the breaks of the Battle River country, the land starts to pitch and roll a bit after steady kilometers of flatland. Bush habitat of poplar and silver willows begins to take over more of the countryside than the carefully tilled, almost perfect geometric shapes of the crop lands. The land is a tapestry of golden ochre fields shaded by sienna borders and pocked with the stands of silver-gray poplars that punch up clumpy spears on the lonely horizon. It's a horizon streaked with splashes of pale vermillion under a deepening canopy of cobalt blue, sometimes etched with clouds and long snaking lines of ravenous mallards swarming the closely cropped fields. Here and there along the way, still tight to daytime cover, we see an occasional whitetail on the edge of the sundown shadows.

This is the land of the biggest whitetails. It doesn't have as many deer as Texas and probably not nearly as many as my home state, Oklahoma. You don't come here for the numbers; you come carrying the dream of a giant, one of those macho, monster, butt-kicking bucks that everyone but you seems to get. But that's not true and you know it. Not everyone gets one of those bucks; actually, hardly anyone does. It just seems that way sometimes. Your honest thought is simply that if you're in the right place at the right time, maybe you will get your chance. It's a dream chase really, a quest for the end of the rainbow where, for a whitetail hunter, the treasure is a hefty handful of beautiful, ivory-tipped bone.

I saw him the first evening. Initially, there was the mere suggestion of movement at the far end of the field. In fading light, bushes become deer, and staring at one spot too long plays games with your head: Kissed by the fading light, a patch of poplar bark is a buck's throat patch, and the branches above turn the patch to a 195 typical. But there is real movement, two blobs turn into moving—that has to be deer—shapes. Zeiss 10x40s suck in the last light from the gloom. He is there. Your breath, even at 200 yards, gets harder to come by, and there's that funny little tremor you experience once in a while running down your right leg. It's hard to hold the glasses steady even when braced against the tree. The first buck is a dream buck, well outside the tips of his ears, upswept main beams colored like fresh, new ivory still seeking the end of his nose in length. He's every bit of a book deer, 20 or more inches on the safe side. You don't give him a second glance.

Big Boy walks up from behind and, as if to prove to anyone watching who has any doubt, rams Junior with a mean upward right from a pile of points (a strong seven, I'm sure) along the highway of a main beam that resembles a tree trunk. He puts things into perspective in his world, and he sends me to dreaming in mine.

I think it's then, in places and situations like that, when we should seriously count our blessings. That day was over, though many more remain. The gods had offered me a gift, a view of the promise that waits at the end of the rainbow. The rest was up to me.

Big bucks are more obvious by the sign they leave than by the fleeting glimpses of their existence. The King lives in a rather small tract of land where the sheds of five singularly different Boone & Crockett bucks have been found in the past 10 years. He is the product of one of those bucks—bucks that were never taken by a hunter. It is surmised, and accurately I suspect, that they all succumbed to the wear and tear of old age in the penetrating cold of an Alberta winter, or to the slashing teeth of hungry coyotes, run to ground on the emptiness of a frozen lake, their final remains, stripped bones and glorious antlers slipping beneath the surface of spring's warming thaw.

I think I saw him once more in the days that followed, though it may well have been another; there wasn't quite enough time to be sure. I was sure only that I was never in the right place at exactly the right time. I saw him though, and while that's not honestly enough—I really wanted him—I can live with the fact that, for a while, I felt I had a chance. ▲

Stalking
Waldo

I named him Waldo. The first two times I saw him, well, he was just a little hard to figure out. My first impression of his horn character made me think of a unicorn, but that wasn't exactly right. It was just that his horns sort of stuck out straight ahead rather than up. Waldo wasn't normal.

His right horn looked a little strange, cork-screwy, curly. It wasn't sticking out as far as the one on the left, but when he turned his head just so, it looked like it might be as long, just bent down in a goofy way.

I saw him for the first time at around nine o'clock on a beautifully clean Colorado morning that was going from warm to hot in a helluva hurry. During the first hour and a half the small water hole in front of my shanty-like box blind had been visited by 21 does and fawns and three yearling bucks that put on a lively show head-butting each other around the pond's perimeter.

The water hole sat on a little bench at the head of a long, narrow valley that widened into a bowl. The bowl was three-quarters of a mile around, rather steep-sided and studded along the upper third with scrubby trees, pines or juniper. It looked exactly like a place a good mule deer buck would pick to spend the summer. Pockets of sage on the sidehill melded with shimmering knee-high golden grass, wiggling on a blessed breeze that funneled up the narrow valley and, fortunately, through the shooting port and peep holes in the blind.

Around 10:30 a.m. the tips of a buck antelope's horns appeared on the scraggly sage skyline in front of the blind. I grabbed up the 10X binocular to check him out, figured him for around 70 inches and put any thought of shooting him from my mind.

When I saw Waldo through the left-hand peep hole, he and another buck were following three does off the sidehill of the bowl. It's hard to get a clean look through a half-inch slit just big enough for one eye—even harder peering through binoculars. All of this simply added to the mystery of just what he was, but I saw enough to know he was different. *He's weird looking,* I thought. *I wish he'd get out where I could have a good look.*

His companions came straight to the water without hesitating, took a brief look about for lions, tigers or whatever antelope think about, then plunged in to suck up enough liquid to carry them through another high desert day. Waldo circled behind the blind, where my vision again was seriously restricted, then bolted and bounced off barking, flaring his rump patch when the shadow of a swooping prairie falcon passed overhead. "Goosy too," I muttered. "A real Waldo." The foursome at the water hadn't even blinked. Yep, Waldo was different.

Along about noon, with the box getting sticky unpleasant, I was thinking pretty hard that the guys back at Phil Phillips' camp were probably sitting in the shade drinking something colder than the tepid remnants in my water bottle. All the water hole was attracting were squabbling flights of magpies, horned larks and a thrush-like bird the prairie falcon tried to turn into breakfast. The thought of something colder than ice, bubbling down my throat, was pulling mighty hard. I copped out and headed for the truck stashed a mile away. Guess what? Standing out in the sage about halfway down the long valley was...yep, there's Waldo.

He was on the edge of that tall yellow-green sage that seems to grow mostly in the lower depressions of the desert. He hadn't seen me—small miracle—because I was just sauntering along a dim, rutted jeep road where he should have seen the cloud of dust I raised. He hadn't. *Hell with it,* I thought. *I gutta go that way, I might as well crawl. If I get close enough (*I didn't expect to), *I'll try to shoot him.*

I had crawled all over Wyoming to shoot my first antelope with a bow—a 49-pound Howard Gamemaster—in 1962. I was reminded of that when I crawled across the first of many ground-hugging cactus to sneak my way to Waldo. Periodically I stretched out on the smoldering sand to rest; I'm not nearly as young as I was in 1962. As I lay there I thought of the antelope I have since shot from a blind. "Blinds make more sense," I muttered, slithering forward. But you know, this sneaking stuff was fun, a neat way to do it. I peeked before flopping over for a sip of my now-hot, dangerously depleted water. Waldo was only about 80 yards away, angling toward me. *This might actually work out,* I thought.

Well, it did. The high green sage had provided some cover. Now Waldo was cutting through it, narrowing the range. I nocked a XX75 and waited.

It was a long, dry walk to the truck, the water bottle hanging bone-dry on my hip. By the time I pulled the dust-encrusted vehicle into camp, I was as parched as one of those sun-bleached range cattle carcasses that litter the western deserts. Lively Leslie Phillips met me at the gate. "We were beginning to worry. How'd you do?" I pointed to the truck bed.

"My, he's weird," she giggled.

"He's not weird. He's Waldo," I croaked. "Where's the cold ones?"

♠

Chapter 9

Friends And Family

Whitetails: Accepting Mediocrity

About a year ago, my good friend, Judd Cooney, wrote the following personal perspective on deer: "I hate whitetails!"

I've considered becoming a disciple of the same persuasion.

It's not that we hate all whitetails, just big whitetails (or anything that scores over 125 inches). Cooney's attitude has mellowed a tad since he penned those words because last season he did in a Pope and Young buck—one of those fabled northern Alberta models that weighs 100 pounds the day it's born. Our effort to grass a book-making flag-waver had been going along quite evenly for the 25 years we've been bushwhacking around North America together. Generally, we've been successful on most everything else and have managed to compile a rather nice list of quality critters in our wanderings. Those experiences count among the most pleasant of my 40 years of bowhunting memories.

Somehow though, my favorite hunting buddy has always

managed to squeak in on top with something slightly better, including one time when he slam-dunked me on antelope. That was eight or nine years ago. Between us we had drawn four pronghorn tags, two apiece for Wyoming and Colorado. In less than a week's time we filled those tags on three bookers that almost measured alike, but the fourth—Judd's—tied the world record! Other than that significant transgression in partnership conduct, we have kept things pretty close.

There was, however, an area where my skills rose to the top. In the matter of whitetails, I had an edge because I hunted them a bit more frequently. I also had the biggest, several of the biggest. In our who-buys-the-drinks contests, that was enough. While I don't know this for sure, I feel comfortable in the notion that this was a key consideration in Judd's building hate-mode regarding whitetails. Let's face it, big whitetails, big being a matter of individual perspective, can certainly tick you off!

Well, Old Judd doesn't hate 'em quite as bad anymore. I know this firsthand because I was on the long-distance receiving end of his hard-earned triumph. It happened last fall, late November if my memory remains correct about events I'd rather not remember. They sent me to bed with a headache. It was late at night in Oklahoma, a cold brutal night with one of our patented Blue Northerns howling around outside, freeze-drying everything from central Kansas south, including a fairly nice chunk of a whitetail that was slowly turning on the gambel hook outside the back door. I was thawing out in front of the television when the phone rang. My wife dragged the receiver across the den, drawing the extension to its limit, with all the coils stretched out taut as a bowstring.

"I think it's Judd," she said, rolling her great green eyes.

It was one of those times when you just know what you're going to hear before you hear it. Cooney has a deep, resonant voice, the kind you'd expect from anyone with a chest the size of a caveman.

"Whaaatareyoudoinn James?" he said. "Trying to catch up with you. You still in Canada?" I answered.

"Yeah, Harvey and I were just sitting here thinking about you." I knew better. They were sitting around in northern Alberta sipping Cooney's favorite mix of Coke, thinking more about how they could ruin my day.

"OK Judson, you have obviously shot something. How big, and what?"

Harvey McNalley's voice cut in on another extension. It sounded like used static. "A whitetail. One-forty-five plus, you miserable flatlander. Whaddaya thing of that, eh?"

"I thing, Harvey, I'll go to bed."

Thus, it came to pass that Cooney slew a trophy whitetail, thereby wrenching the ring from my stretched fingers as he once again slid into Victory Lane ahead of me. Although I was honestly tickled for him, I was beginning to wonder and seriously assess my own position in the big whitetail picture. I had spent 56 hours in tree stands and ground blinds hunting McNalley's fabled Alberta whitetails and never even saw a buck. I take that back. I almost ran over one when I was driving back to camp after dark. He was a big one, too. Does that count?

This big-whitetail thing is getting to me. I mean fair-and-square big whitetails. There's a lot of hanky-panky going on in the whitetail world today that's tarnishing the game, but that's another subject. I'd rather bare my soul by discussing my own ineptitude, which has to do with bad luck, bad timing, bad planning, bad weather, and some bad shooting. Mostly I prefer to blame it on luck, or a lack of it.

It's not too bad a deal though. People are beginning to take pity on me. In the last few years I have been invited on more trophy whitetail ventures than I can honestly accept. The reasoning is simple if you look at it from an outfitter's perspective. "Hey, if we can get Dougherty a book whitetail, everyone in the world will just have to realize what a great place we have, so let's invite the poor snake-bit bowman on a hunt!"

So far it's been great. I have seen a lot of fine whitetail country, even a few dream deer, and met a lot of good people, but on only one occasion have I had a chance at a big deer, which, in complete honesty, I missed. Did it bother me? Of course not. The hunt's the thing, the outdoor experience. It is only important to have hunted. That was four years ago, and I still wake up screaming. However, it didn't bother me....

It's really kind of funny, as in peculiar, how big this whole whitetail thing has become. Wherever I go, to a speaking engagement at Anderson's International Bowhunter's Clinic for instance, they will come up and ask, "Did you get a big buck last year?" "Hey Jim, did you get him?" You see, they know just how very high the odds are of ever seeing a Pope and Young whitetail in most of the country, and how very, very high the odds are against collecting one. Sure, some guys do it regularly, most on an upfront basis. It's nice to have them out there, as they blow us the breath of hope.

Well, I'm not going to worry about it any more than I have for the last God-only-knows-how-many seasons. It's not that I don't do a pretty good number on whitetails, only that the number on a particular buck someplace hasn't come up on my own lottery ticket. Do I think it ever will? Yes! I have to, even though I'll be reasonably content to roll along forever in white-tail mediocrity if it doesn't. You see, most bowhunters won't hit the jackpot either. Even some of the foremost names in the land will never catch the whitetail ring. But, Cooney did. That's good enough for me. He didn't really mean it when he said he hated them, and I never will hate them either. In fact, I love the challenge they present. ⚐

Friends

The deer season here is nearly a third over as I reflect on things while watching the fox squirrel who's watching back at me through my open window. It's a bright clean day, cool with a southwesterly breeze. I should be in a stand or scouting—not here, looking through a window at a semi-tame squirrel that has cautiously started to trust me. The last days of October are winding down, and I found three fresh scrapes yesterday along the edge line of the woods that run close by the comfy stand in one of my favorite places.

The acorns are skimpy this year, which is good because I found a little pocket of oaks that's loaded, which is kinda like knowing the location of the only restaurant in town. I put a new stand up covering one main trail leading to it and figure it needs another for when the winds turn and go north. Things are cook'n, the good times are ready to roll; I should be out hunt'n instead of watching my semi-tame squirrel. That's okay, I'm thinking about what's happened already and what's next!

So far the season's been good, since antelope camp last

July, then mule deer and elk moved on into September. I didn't get an elk, though I think I really could have, and the mule deer's nothing extra special until you put him on a plate. Everything's gone smoothly and nothing bad's really happened, though there were 10 days in Quebec looking for caribou and not seeing a single one (!) that stretched my enthusiasm mighty thin.

Hunting migrating caribou in northern Quebec can be pretty iffy. You have to accept that going in and go with the right partner. I went with an old buddy who's been around the hunting block more times than he probably remembers. George Gardner's bowhunted the round world over and understands that there will be times when things simply don't click and won't come together. He doesn't bitch, rant or whine, or blame the outfitter or lousy weather for it.

My friend knew that Quebec's caribou migrations are fickle and that they're goofier than a yard full of tame turkeys and move only when they're damn good and ready. He understood that he didn't buy a caribou, only a chance, like a lottery ticket (though we both felt the odds were much better).

Ten days of staring over miles of caribou-less caribou moss, pine trees and water through low-scudding clouds and misty, cold rain didn't dampen our appreciation of the experience and beauty of the land, nor—though being bored nearly stiff with inactivity—our pleasure of being together.

Situations like that are bound to happen, especially in remote areas. You're in much more of a pickle than being somewhere in Colorado or Montana because, quite simply, you're stuck! You can't drive or walk out, and the float plane won't come to get you just because you're bored, though it will if you can pop a grand or two extra for a ticket. Over time I've been on some bad, loser doozies, trips where the hunting or conditions were sour, sometimes even dangerous. But invariably I've been with close friends, partners who can go with the flow, who find humor in any situation and are there to get you out of a jam.

While I enjoy the solitude of actually hunting and being

alone, I treasure the travel and camp life with my family and friends even more. Each year I map out the coming season's plans based on who can go, more than where or for what, and my memory is colored with people in past places as much if not more than anything we shot.

I guess that sums up my strongest feelings when it comes to hunting. In my youth the desire to succeed burned pretty deep (as it does in all of us, I'm sure) but it never overrode the enjoyment or importance of being there, doing it and having fun with my friends. Sure, it was often competitive—getting the biggest, shooting better, winning first place meant something—but it wasn't about beating your buddies as much as sharing a rocking good time.

As the years pass, ties with old friends maintain their importance, though occasions to hunt together may diminish as life's course takes its quirky twists and turns. And while they might stretch some, the ties holding true friends never break. More frequently now, as we grow older, a friend may go away forever and you recall the good times by campfires and hope he knows you're thinking about him from his place up there in the stars.

Yep, so far it's been a good season from the Colorado camps to wind-swept Quebec and the bright fall-colored crispness of Michigan and Wisconsin, and more is still to come. I'm thinking now about the little stand of fertile oaks and the rich, round nuts there dropping on the ground, and that my other George buddy, George Wright, is coming from California next week. I need to remember he shoots a recurve right-handed when I put up more stands, and to change angle on the comfy stand.

I'm thinking of two other places I need to look over where good bucks have run in the past. The mission is a whitetail; George has never got one, and it won't matter much if he doesn't. We'll hunt pretty hard and take things as they come like we have for the last 40 years. It will be another great week in a very good season of just going bowhunting with friends. ▲

Partners
In
Time

The once snappy, pitch-rich fire had burned down to a comfortable level when he appeared at the edge of the soft, golden light. There was no sound of his approach; he was just suddenly there. "Hello," he said. "Uuh, hullo," someone replied, almost cautiously.

"You bowhunting?" he questioned, stepping noiselessly into the full flickering light. He was a young guy (older than me at 17) with wide, powerful shoulders and a narrow waist. His big hands held an unstrung bow.

"Sure are, you done any good?"

"Nope, bowstring broke, wondered if you might have an extra."

I will forever recall that in the neat camp nestled tight into an aspen grove in Red's Meadow, in the California Sierras—on the occasion of our first real bowhunt away from home—we did not. I recall it because we had a dozen bowstrings of different lengths, but not one to fit the quiet stranger's bow. He carried a solid fiberglass recurve. If my memory serves it was a Ben

Pearson model #336 at 50 pounds. I would ask him that today, but I cannot.

I was a high schooler then working at Doug Kittredge's famous Bow Hut. One Saturday months later, a fellow walked in, smiled and said, "I finally found a string." He explained that he had driven, town by town, all the way back to Bakersfield before he found a bowstring. He had returned to Red's Meadow the next day. I calculated that as a 700-mile round-trip! The "Sierras" name we placed on everything along the eastern slope from Lone Pine to Bridgeport, California, had a fine mule deer population then. It is meaningless to lament over what has happened to them, except to say that very few remain.

The meaningful part of this recollection is that Saturday I met George Kili. Though a dozen years separated our ages, it was apparent we shared interests well beyond our relatively new fascination with archery. Kili was a fisherman, upland bird hunter, waterfowler, varmint caller and rifleman. Bowhunting was new to him. Truth is, in 1954, it was new to all of us. Not one of our combined acquaintances, except for Jack Howard, had ever shot a deer with a bow.

By nature, Kili was pretty much a loner. I have often thought it unusual that a man nearing middle age, and a kid (by comparison) would form a bowhunting partnership that could last more than 40 years. It really all began with chuckars.

On the steep, almost bare foothills at the south end of the San Joaquin Valley, years of effort by the California Dept. of Fish & Game had established huntable populations of chuckar partridge. Like most game that thrived in California, Kili knew where to find them. He invited me to try them with him, said he'd call when the season opened and left the shop. I didn't hear from him until the following fall.

"Lo Jim, George Kili, ready to try some chuckar?" We filled many limits of chuckar and plump valley quail. We pursued bandtailed pigeons in the high country, pheasants in cotton fields and weed-choked bar pits of the central valley and spent, Lord only knows, how many hours in duck blinds, goose pits and fishing boats. We became pards.

Our true bond, though, was always bowhunting. Kili became one of the best bowhunters I will ever know. Blinded in the right eye at an early age by a fragment of brass from a blown 30.06 case, he shot left-handed. He could see better with one eye than most people ever do with two. We took our first bow-and-arrow deer the same year, smallish California mulies. Back then just bowhunting for deer was an adventure; getting one was a dream. It's fair to say now that it wasn't too long before our dreams became regular reality. As our skills improved, our horizons broadened.

We ranged farther afield, thinking about bigger deer in interesting places—Nevada, Utah, Idaho and Arizona's famed Kaibab Plateau. It didn't take long before Kili's name became synonymous with big bucks. Bowhunters knew of him from the dark, friendly little bar of the Jarbidge Club in far north-eastern Nevada to the bright neons at Jacobs Lake on the plateau.

In that era—the 1960s—when bowhunting was beginning to come of age, George Kili was already full grown. One after-noon, on a long, second gear grade grinding slowly from the valley upwards to Jarbidge, Nevada, we stopped for a truck full of bowhunters lumbering down. I asked what success they were having. "Well, George Kili got a 30-incher yesterday. You know who he is?"

I grinned. "Yeah, I sure do!"

There was a lot of the spirit of the mountain man in this hunter. He had no problem being alone, hunting alone. It fit his temperament and style like the way he set out to hunt cougar. On a cold, nasty winter's day, with one dog, three arrows and treacherous, back-breaking hip-deep snow, he got two!

In '71 I left California for Oklahoma. For almost every fall that followed, Kili came to Tulsa for whitetails, waterfowl, and Sue's cooking. Sometimes he came in the late spring, too, for the bass-fishing lessons my son Kelly laid on him. He made a wild bowhunting float trip in Alaska with my oldest son, Jim, who for some reason christened him "The Royal Gorge". It fit, stuck hard and stayed.

I could never account for the days we spent together, the downed deer and elk we wrestled with, the arrows and shotshells we shot. There are vivid memories: the triple he made on green winged teal burning by on a screecher of a tail wind; the perfectly heart-shot eight pointer that ran for 100 yards to pile up 10 yards from my stand. Mostly, though, I remember the elk hunts. Elk were his favorite game, the mountains his favorite environment.

We spoke last September and he was not doing very well health-wise. But he talked about making it to Oklahoma in October. Whitetail hunting wouldn't be too tough he thought. I agreed. We'd fix up his favorite stand; it was still a hot spot, I said.

"Goin' elk hunting?" he asked.

"Yeah, leaving tomorrow. Want to come along?"

He kind of chuckled and said no, he didn't think so, just get one, and save him the best steak.

As you probably figured, he didn't make Oklahoma in October. He left while I was on that elk hunt, freed of the frustrating pain he handled quietly, like most everything he dealt with. And weeks later on a clean, cool October evening with the coals getting just right, I thought, Royal Gorge, you were one helluva pardner, and I'm going to eat your steak.

In my head the phone was ringing. "Lo Jim, George. Wanna' try some chuckars?" ⚑

Rendezvous

Many years ago, the Mountain Men trappers and hunters would gather at places like Bear Lake on today's Idaho-Wyoming border after long periods of dangerous, oftentimes solitary existence. Some came from extraordinary distances on foot, others by horse, funneling from remote rolling plains and high lonesome valleys to the place they called "Rendezvous." There they met old friends, and for a period of a few weeks traded, hunted, swapped stories and caroused in the companionship of their fellows ,though it's said that they were soon just as eager to return to their reclusive wild ways as they were to attend.

I've been thinking about a "rendezvous" quite a bit lately, certainly not the same, though in some ways not very different, and certainly not one I'll be anxious to leave—a meeting with old friends I haven't seen in quite a while in a lovely green valley in northwest Colorado. Thinking and planning for it has helped me through the summer.

I don't mean to offend anyone who likes Oklahoma summers, for nine months I truly love Oklahoma. However, to me, early summer mornings when the birds first start talking and the grass in the yard is heavy with dew is the only part of summer worth saving. June for the most part, and for sure all of July doesn't do much at all for my mood, early August either. It's too hot, too humid, too buggy a time here with not much to do. Oh, I'll hit the ox bows off the Verdigris River with a buddy an hour or so before first light now and then, tossing topwater chuggers and jerk baits for bass. I love to lay out gaudy deer hair bugs I've tied on a seven weight fly rod and twitch them to life, hoping something will take. But when the rising sun glares hot red through summer's humid haze on oppressive still mornings, well, the rest of the day's gonna be downright unpleasant! Most summer mornings I'll be out in the yard shooting my bow in the cool early light. I don't shoot many arrows and not at all fast, just a very casual pace between sips of fresh coffee trying to concentrate on smooth draw and aiming, something I trust will help later when it has to be quick and automatic. I shoot more broadheads than field points into a foam target; by August it's in tatters and goes out with the trash.

Getting ready for rendezvous, practicing, gathering gear helps pass the time, and I always make up a batch of new arrows for every new season. My wife finds this strange 'cause the garage is full of carefully racked arrows—no less than 30 dozen—and some would be perfect in the new bow I'm shooting, but she's missing the point: new season, new arrows, it's the right thing to do! Gathering up gear from clothing to game bags begins with a checklist, at the top, underlined in red letters is written "license & tags." Once I went to rendezvous and left my deer tag at home. Finding all the stuff on my check list requires quite a search, I know that I have it, just not where I put it, or who might have borrowed something I need. Gathering new gear is the fun part. I wear out the pages of my latest master catalog looking for new things I want. Truth be known, I don't need a darn thing, though I will find something I want. It's a "he-who-dies-with-the-most-toys-wins" kinda thing. I don't expect to win, but I do want to be in the race.

This rendezvous is targeted to mule deer and elk at Jay Verzuh's camp with maybe a crack at a bear and surely some blue grouse to sweeten the pot, yet it's much more than just hunting; this meeting of friends is the core of what our bowhunting's about. There's George Wright and Bruce Hendy, partners of more than 40 years, "Judge" Pete of course, though not nearly for as long, and Jay and I have teamed up for near 25. I have no accurate recollection of how many hunts, days and nights I've shared with these men, how many stalks Jay and I've made, how many gobblers Pete and I have chased, but I recall many places and events. The big bull elk Bruce took in Sawmill Canyon: fretting 'cause he didn't think he'd hit it right, hell, it was straight through the heart! George's bull moose as the weather shut down the Alaskan Peninsula and the bush pilot was lost (crashed, it turned out), the dog that ran off with his antelope horns in Wyoming (a "booker") and the dog's still alive 'cause we found them! Pete's first bull elk from the stand at Quaking Springs: misjudged the yardage, hit him dead center! Hmm, How'd he make that work? Early 1960s in Arizona's Kiabab when Wright and I had three deer and all our gear in (on) his Triumph TR-3! Bruce chest deep in a frigid Alberta river retrieving his moose. Ever tried to retrieve a sunken moose? Midday shade under the cottonwoods will provoke countless recollections of good days and bad, a few even dangerously scary, and though sometimes things were testy, I can't recall a serious harsh word one said to another.

Don't be misled, this is not about a bunch of old guys lying about in the shade reliving old glories. There are big bucks and bulls there, and that's what we're after, though "trophies" are not so all-important anymore. A fat cow elk is a very good deal, a batch of tender blue grouse makes a helluva camp meal. Yeah, the rendezvous is coming, the cool high country's waiting. We're all gathered and packed, we're ready to roll. ▲

Chapter 10

Deer With White Tails

Doing
Time In
A Tree

Ice-encased oak leaves plummeted in deadfall spirals like hard-shot ducks down to the worn, weather-roughened redwood picnic table. They clattered a steady tattoo on the roofs of our base-camp trailers. It was one of those calm, soggy mornings where the air was thick enough to see hanging and shifting in a kind of surreal, clammy curtain of gloom. This was not to our collective minds our favorite kind of day.

I know people who prefer days like these for hunting deer, days that are in my opinion better reserved for waterfowling. My experiences have never been good enough in this kind of climactic goop to feel that it offered better-than-average odds. This may be because I have a tendency to give up and climb down from my stand earlier than usual in this kind of weather, an obvious flaw in my makeup, for I know as well as anyone that sticking to it is what it takes.

In any case, this was one of the glummer days, the nastiest of the year. None of us who was hunkered deep in our collars around the old table had seen anything this particular morning—nothing. It was just another nail in the coffin of what was not turning out to be a good year. Not only was our take way down overall, better than half the usual average for the camp, but sightings had been fewer, too. Good bucks seemed to be almost, if not completely, nonexistent. We mulled over the possible reasons repeatedly: The impact of herbicide spraying? A lack of proper forage? A poor mast crop? Some biological fingers were beginning to point toward what at first had begun as merely a notion; that a die-off, cause as yet undetermined, had banged up our herd.

Cold, clammy mornings with no action, one after another, become the true test of a bowhunter's optimism. With many tags having gone unfilled and those brand-new hollow freezers glaring in cavernous loneliness at home, it was, as one who had recently bought one put it (he had filled all five tags the previous year) "unnecessary to have subscribed to the service contract."

Late-morning gatherings are usually interesting. Most of us share factual information. Others, as if worried someone else might run across their spot, don't. On a day like this, near the end of a slow season, and this in the peak of the good time, optimism was grinding to a slow halt, a stage approaching defeat, and an unheard-of attitude among us loomed.

To be perfectly honest, tree-stand hunting is not nearly my favorite cup of tea. I really don't care for it, even though some of the most exciting moments of my life have taken place while living them from the perspective of a squirrel. It's akin to the description a friend of mine, a commercial pilot, uses to define his job; hours upon hours of pure boredom interrupted by the occasional moment of sheer terror. The parallel seems rather appropriate.

At heart I'm a wandering, go-for-a-look-see kind of hunter when I have a bow in my hand. I would ten times rather shoot one deer from the ground than several from a tree, just as I would rather shoot one decoying duck than jump-shoot a dozen. It's simply a matter of personal preference.

Like most bowhunters, the greatest portion of my annual

hunting time is spent in pursuit of whitetail deer. Whitetails, like it or not, are most effectively hunted from tree stands. So there you are.

Steam from our coffee mugs barely made a dent in the soupy atmosphere that lay heavy with a humidity load that neared 100 percent. The drizzle, approaching snow but as yet unsure just exactly what it really wanted to become, pummeled our dampened spirits. It was on this note that the conversation turned to the tedium we experience while sitting on stand.

My son Kelly has forsaken wearing a watch while sitting in wait. Its presence only heightens the doldrums of waiting, when waiting seems to be the only thing that he will end up doing. I wear one and have perfected the art of looking at it exactly every half hour, give or take no more than a minute. It is as if the sweeping hands are in my head and not on my wrist. I will say to myself in a whisper, "It must be eight o'clock," and it will be.

My hunting companions and I have various methods for passing time. Several of us will take a paperback novel to a stand, most often if we plan to spend an extra-long time sitting, as we are inclined to do when the rut is in full swing. (More big bucks fall at midday than you can imagine.) I used to take novels on occasion. This was before I was saddled with wearing bifocals for up-close vision. They do not work well if you leave them on and have to shoot in a hurry. The result will be a guaranteed miss. On a hunt in Michigan I switched to those little granny-style reading glasses, the kind that dangle precariously on the end of your nose. You can't see beyond the pages of a book with them, which means you must remove them when you check out the little out-of-place leaf rustling that you heard off to the right. I gave up taking novels many seasons ago.

Marking time is achieved in a variety of ways. According to George Bennett, a big burly guy who's as long on patience as a buzzard, it takes seven and a half minutes for the sugar coating on an M&M to totally dissolve in the corner of your mouth. That equates to 32 M&M's for a normal four-hour stint.

Carrying that notion further, I noted that a Jolly Roger—watermelon flavor—will vanish in 13 minutes when you simply hold it in place, which is almost impossible to do. Rolling it around in your mouth reduces the time it takes to dissolve by half.

For me, earplug radios are out of the question; still, music will run through my head repeatedly. This season a continuous stream of Garth Brooks' ballads "turned on" as soon as my silent vigil began. Radios, though, are the norm on Saturdays for some Oklahoma bowhunters. They cannot bear to pass the afternoon ignorant of OU's fate.

I cannot tolerate anything that remotely interferes with my ability to hear and sort out the sounds of the woods. I know I hear 90 percent of my deer before I ever see them. No, electronic crutches are not for me. The music that plays in my head as the hard candy rolls around in my mouth will have to do if any extra help is needed to pass the time.

Toward noon, there is a suggestion of a break in the weather. The sun doesn't really come out; we just know it's up there somewhere. The light is brighter to the southwest, and the wind is shifting.

The break affects our spirits and gives us a sense of renewed energy. We think a climatic break will make the deer move. The afternoon will be good. This reaction runs chainlike throughout the camp. Optimism is restored, though not totally.

"You know," said Bennett as he headed for his mud-encrusted Blazer, "it takes 53 minutes to melt a baby Snickers down to nothing but the peanuts. Catch!"

I snatched the miniature brown-wrapped missile from the air and headed for my truck.   ♠

Timing
Is
Everything

Last September, a month before the season opened, I located two nice whitetail bucks frequenting my favorite Oklahoma hunting spot. The first time I saw them the larger deer, an eight pointer, still carried tattered strands of velvet. His companion, a buck of equal body size, had a smaller 10-point rack that was rubbed out and polished. Neither deer was quite big enough to make the book, which gave me confidence. I'm hell on subminimum bucks.

Regardless of antler size, these were experienced deer, veterans of several seasons of serious hunting pressure. While my spot is located on private land, the deer travel onto public ground to feed on a state-managed public hunting area. The unit is farmed with wheat, soybeans and milo—irresistible groceries. So, like all whitetails that go where their stomachs lead them, they take chances. By doing so, they run afoul with archery hunters, muzzleloaders and riflemen in season, and sadly, poachers year-round. Like whitetails everywhere, they get sharp in a real hurry.

Six years of hunting this little spot had provided me with a heck of an education in wind and whitetails. It took awhile to understand it, and in the process I spooked some good bucks. I just didn't believe what the fickle tendrils of human-laden scent could do on this little crown of a hill. Eventually, I realized what conditions would beat the keen noses of deer. Once I realized and accepted them—resisting the temptation to hunt when conditions were marginal—I knew I had things as much under human control as possible.

It wasn't that you couldn't hunt the area under marginal conditions; you could, and with a reasonable chance for success, too. The point is doing it right, maximizing the location's potential without spooking an experienced deer—the deer you want. Over the years, before I understood just how things worked, I had been good at spooking deer there. The two bucks I saw in September were the best in the area. I wanted to hunt them very carefully.

Everything seemed right the first morning I tried. On the way in, I puffed out half a bottle of powder and a double handful of milkweed chaff as I went. The drift looked perfect. Thirty minutes into the morning the light breeze shifted. I saw the subtle suggestion in the pattern of milkweed blooms as they turned their dance downhill. I was stiffed and knew it. There was nothing to do but bail out. My watch said there was time—these deer are remarkably predictable—so I left, cutting across the prairie to a spot where I could watch without fouling my place.

At 8:10 a.m. both bucks, along with three does, one fawn and a spike, walked by the stand in single file at 15 yards. I steadied the Zeiss 10X on each buck before they vanished into the waist-high bluestem. Very nice. I'd take either one.

The wind was wrong the next morning, so I drove out on the prairie to a vantage point a mile away to watch. My two bucks were still together, sparring a bit, their necks noticeably swelling. The eight pointer made a move on an unreceptive doe that scampered off. At 7:45 a.m. they moved out of sight. I knew where they were going.

When I checked outside the trailer in the predawn of the following morning, the wind had shifted under a silver, cloudless sky. It seemed right, but you can't really tell from down in the valley. Stirring my coffee, I told my wife, "If it's like this at the top of Bull Meadow, I should get a chance around 8:15." As I went out the door her "good luck!" response was muffled by the pillows.

It's a bone-jarring four-mile drive and mile-long walk angling uphill through tall bluestem prairie grass to the stand. I stopped twice to double-check the wind. Perfect. I was getting pumped. The stand fits in a stubbly blackjack oak only eight feet high. Its swivel seat has been gnawed around the edges by the male fox squirrel that lives in the second oak to the south. The seat swivels smoothly, dead-quiet. I have shot all my deer but two from this stand while sitting down; most of them were standing within yards of the same place. It's a super setup, but it's the kind of place where you have to pay close attention: When the deer come through, they are usually in a hurry.

As with any setup you think is perfect, there's always a time that will prove it's not. Two seasons ago, on a chilly November morning, I was watching shimmering glimpses of a deer moving toward me to my right. Clean sunlight filtering through a lacework of branches reflected splatters of white and golden tan highlights. It was easy to watch the deer without really seeing it. A leg moved, the flash of a white throat patch, a flickering tail— all glistened to mark its progress. It was a doe. I felt she should have a buck somewhere in tow. She did. He was there, a phantom at nine o'clock. Nine o'clock deer for a left-hander sitting down are impossible! I didn't even try. He walked out of my life, a fine 10 pointer I believe would have scored in the 130s. I had never seen him before, nor have I since.

This morning a lone fawn, a little button buck with fuzzy knobs, came through at 8 a.m. Twelve yards, oblivious. Some minutes passed, then rustling leaves put me on point. Three does moving fast. I shifted on the swivel seat, but they eased by, intent on their distant bedding ground. If you do this a lot you learn to rely on your ears as much as anything. The clicking noise was subtle, different. I wasn't sure. Sound drew my eyes to the point of origin. There was movement: antler tips rubbing a branch. It was the eight pointer paralleling the does.

Then came the hard part: a deer approaching that you plan to shoot. It's the toughest part of the game. I was turned, ready to draw, my mind running through all the things I had to do to do it well, my right toe pressing down on the stand to keep the tremor running up my leg in check. It always does that when I'm on a stand, waiting, knowing I'm going to shoot. It's an adrenaline rush. I like it!

I drew as his head passed behind a tree, followed him for three steps and released when his left leg moved forward. He was gone in a flash, turning back downhill in a churning dash. Before he was out of sight, I could tell he was losing his balance.

I looked at my watch—8:15 a.m.

Big Buck Luck

This matter of big whitetails seems like one of those epidemics that sweeps across continents. Maybe hysteria is a better description. I'm not quite sure why; I just know it has all the indicators of both.

Now, I confess to a high level of interest. I truly enjoy hunting whitetails, and I am certainly interested in collecting a really good one before I cash in all my chips. I expect I will. It's a thought I hold onto and something I plan a great deal of my fall hunting schedule around.

I have had my chances at several big whitetails and have failed. I have also met a few that never gave me a chance. I think that's the way it is supposed to be. Bowhunting is like that, at least for me. I make no excuses for clean misses, which, of course, are disappointing. What really irks me is luck—or the lack of it, if you will.

Years ago, Fred Bear and I were reviewing a display of awesome whitetails at the Pope & Young biennial convention in Boise—bucks that were the best of the previous two-year recording period. We were seriously impressed. "Seen many like these, Fred?" I asked. He swept the display with his piercing eyes, sort of hunching his lanky frame to take a good, hard look. "No," he replied. "You know, I don't believe I have ever seen an honest 125-inch buck when I was hunting whitetails. Never been lucky enough!"

At that time, in the twilight of his years, Fred had done it all. Maybe not by today's high-tech, easier-to-do criteria; but in my book, based on the standards of his era and most of mine—time, travel, tactics, techniques and equipment—he had. Fred had hunted whitetails all his life. He was instrumental in my introduction to them, providing no small amount of good advice in that initial exposure. He knew what it was all about, yet not only had he never taken a big one, he wasn't sure he'd ever even seen one! The nice thing about that was, it didn't bother him. He wasn't a victim of the red-eyed obsession so common today.

A few years later, at the Pope & Young convention in Tulsa, we did the same sort of walk-through. The display of gigantic whitetails was even more impressive—as they are inclined to be with each passing year. Fred talked about whitetails then in a different perspective. It was his opinion, a point he made several times in my presence, that whitetail deer would become one of bowhunting's salvations. They were becoming extremely "convenient", and bowhunting would become one of the most effective management tools for controlling their rapidly expanding numbers near urban areas. Well, the whitetail has indeed become "convenient", and I think Fred's prophecy will soon be true if it is not already.

"Trophy" whitetails have become big business, fostering no small number of fringe industries in the shooting sports. Some are quite good; others are ridiculously inane. They have spawned a few high-profile careers, and sadly they have led to the destruction of others. Mostly, though, they have disrupted countless hours of restful sleep with toss-and-turn dreams or nightmares for almost every archery hunter east of Nevada. Some people I have known for years—common, careful, normal folks—have gone off the deep end of life's pool because of whitetails. I am sadly aware of the termination of several marriages brought about by whitetails, one the direct result of a brother-in-law taking a "Big One". Hubby couldn't handle it. He should have talked to me about it sooner. I know of places, fair-chase places, too, where he could have gone and gotten one for three or four grand—a heck of a lot less expensive than the cost of a lovely family, as if such things have a price. But then, I reckon if he'd spent the money, the results might have been the same.

I am a little bit critical of this entire big whitetail thing. It seems that's all we see, hear or read about. Every magazine features them almost exclusively on their covers.

Maybe I'm getting too crotchety in my old age, bored with too much media hype and expert secrets. I confess to being susceptible, too. You see, like everyone who lives near them—and the greatest percentage of our nation's hunters do—I spend more time hunting whitetails than anything else. I have bowhunted since I was 14 in a lot of fabulous places, some very far from home, and I still do. Yet every year I spend more time hunting whitetails than all other game combined, including turkeys, which my wife will confirm is an obsession. One reason, of course, is that whitetails are very convenient for me, and I do like to hunt them.

The main reason, though, is that I'm just like everyone else: I want a big one, too. I admit to wanting one pretty badly, but not more than anything else. I am not obsessed by it, and given a choice, I'd really rather have a huge bull elk. I look on this as an exercise in determination that helps mold my character. Success eventually comes to those who stick it out—I just wonder if I'll live long enough. Occasionally I reflect on my blown opportunities, rationalizing that I was lucky to have had the chance to have just seen one.

I think that when it happens, when I finally catch up to the Big One (which really doesn't have to be too big), then things will all come together. After that, because I will get back to a more relaxed whitetail hunting attitude, I will probably stumble across a couple of others. This will make me a sort of minor guru.

All in all, the element of luck Fred alluded to has as much to do with nailing a big whitetail as anything. If you don't have some luck once in awhile, you're in for a tough time indeed. Sure, there are legitimate whitetail hunting phenomenons like Gene and Barry Wensel or Myles Keller, who knock off the big ones with a regularity that turns everyone green. That's life. There is always someone, somewhere in any field of endeavor who consistently gets it all together—not every time, just often enough. They are blessed with something extra special that separates them, and each will admit to having an extra helping of luck.

Collecting a big whitetail is only a dream for most of us. Like Fred, most of us never will. We might not ever even see one, yet our daily lives will continue to be saturated with the how-to messages that tell us we can. Maybe that's good. After all, we all need some sugar to spice up our dreams. ♠

Sitting In Kansas

The annual rumor that Kansas would soon allow nonresident deer hunting came around again in 1994 like it had for the past two years. It was enough to fire up the dreams and imaginations of serious whitetail hunters across the Midwest, maybe even the entire country. A fellow I know as far away as New York was ecstatic about the possibility.

Of course, we had heard that song before. It was supposedly a "done deal" in 1993, but it hadn't happened. Oklahoma had drawn a line with both Iowa and Kansas that year, telling bowhunters from both states that they couldn't trip south and shoot Okie deer. I don't think that really created too much of a stir with the masses, although I heard some Kansas bigwigs with lots of Oklahoma real estate were mighty irked. Political pressure? Maybe. Who knows?

The rumor mill got hotter during the spring when the official word was handed down. Yes, indeed, the Land of Dorothy and Toto was throwing open its gates—well, cracking them anyhow, to the tune of slightly more than 1,000 archery, firearm and muzzleloader permits combined. Personally, I looked at it as a mere tidbit, sort of a "throw 'em a bone" kind of thing, though some likened it to The Second Coming.

What's that old line? Hope springs eternal...! So, like everyone who dreams straw-stack fantasies, I decided to take my chances in what was perceived to be a drawing with odds significantly greater than those for winning the California Lottery. But, if there was a chance to snatch the brass ring and draw the coveted ticket, I figured I'd better go for it. Honestly, I didn't think I had a prayer. I imagined Kansas would be inundated with the greatest crush of applications from whitetail fanatics in the history of the world. Ah, well, damn the price—which was pretty steep. I went for it!

I opted for the Buddy Application approach with Dave "Balanced Bowhunting" Holt and Tim Yandell, a good friend with a Kansas land connection—an item worth serious consideration in a tightly private state. We would apply for a unit with only 55 archery permits. I did the necessary paperwork, sent it off and promptly put it from my mind. I never win anything.

"Guess what?" My wife dropped an envelope bearing the return address of the Kansas Department of Wildlife & Parks in front of me.

"Well, I'll be. And I know exactly where the Yellow Brick Road starts, too, right over there in the good old sedan. Gads, glad I didn't get one for Iowa."

"Me, too. I'd like to have you around sometime this fall."

"Tell you what, Sugar. I'll make it a point to be here for Thanksgiving."

"You'd better, or I'll cook your goose instead of a turkey!"

So, I started cranking up for another wishful assault, this time in flat ol' Kansas. It really isn't as flat or as dull as some folks make it out to be. Kansas is a land of prime habitat for game both big and small. Huge mule deer roam the western part with their whitetail cousins. Incidentally, this part of the state was not included in the 1994 drawing, except for a white-tails-only area in a small, northwestern corner. The bulk of the available permits were for six eastern management units, but, heck, it was a beginning, and Tim's early scouting reports were getting my always optimistic blood up. "Jim, there's lots of good deer on this place."

So, what happened? Well, it's still too soon to tell. You see, it's still November as I write this. The weather has been yo-yoing from really rotten to almost okay. A few mornings have barely teased the 40-degree mark, with daytime temperatures as warm as they are in summer. Recently, the wind has been hard from the south in excess of 25 miles per hour.

Last evening, I was sitting on the tailgate waiting for Dave to come in. The truck was parked at the edge of an alfalfa field that sparkled with a blinking array of fireflies. Fireflies in November! I mused. This is really weird!

The place we're hunting is jammed full with deer, too damn many really. Too many does with young ones mixed with goofy freshman and twitchy junior-size bucks. Stiff as it is with deer, the swirling, fickle wind has beaten us up pretty good. It's one of those interesting, tactical problems that are tricky to figure out, although, honestly, we could have smacked several okay bucks if we were in a hurry. Tim did one in right off the bat on a pattern he figured out before the October 1 opening. Dave figures he had the right idea; good, late-summer buck patterns can be pretty reliable. It's hard for us to get in a rush. History and experience have taught us what will happen real soon: The does will get romantic and trigger a raunchy buck explosion.

We are hunting prairie deer in rolling country of vast grassland pastures. The fencerows are lined with awesome Osage orange trees as tall as any I've ever seen. They bend under a magnum crop of the yellow-green softball-size "oranges". Deer nibble on them with a rather disinterested attitude. There is new, lush green wheat sown in the wider draws and the alfalfa, which should have frosted yellow by now, is still pretty perky. A winding main creek cuts the property, and a handful of trickling drainages meet it every now and then. The waterways support a hodgepodge of hackberry, elm, hickory, sycamore, plum, some cedar and a bunch of stuff I should know the names of but don't. I haven't found any form of oak on the place. I'm sure five bucks

I have seen will "book" easily; certainly the one I want to meet will, with his high, ivory-white, wide-sweeping 10 points. He's a beauty; just seeing him has been worth the price of admission.

A few days remain before Thanksgiving, and rainy, cooler weather is in the forecast. I'll have to quit soon. I've got to be home for the holidays or get my goose cooked!

"You're coming back, aren't you?" Dave asked.

"Soon as I can, early December probably. What about you? Staying?"

"Yeah, I'm stayin'. Until Christmas, if I have to."

I guess some guys don't have a goose cooker to worry about.

♠

Ten-Minute
Whitetail

A t the edge of the creek where the cattle trail dropped
off steeply into treacherous, inky gloom I struggled
to shrug off my daypack. Slipping the pack on over
all my layers of clothing had been a chore; taking it off was a
job to task Houdini. Why hadn't I had the sense to pull out
the flashlight earlier?

The pack finally fell free as a gust of frigid wind blew my
hat skittering onto the murky prairie, where 18-inch
bluestem grass lay flat and crunchy under a shimmering coat
of ice. "North winds 20 to 25 with gusts up to 35 miles per
hour. High today 32." The TV weatherman had offered that
prognosis with a mildly apologetic look as if to say, sorry for
you folks that have to go outside.

I probed the grass and located my cap milliseconds
before my ears froze off. Ooh, they burned. Holding the bow
by the string rather than clutch its painfully cold riser, I
scanned the rock- strewn gloomy void where the icy trail wandered to the frozen creek. "This," I had thought, while con-

Deer With White Tails 177

templating my treadless felt-lined boots, "is not smart!" Yet who says that bowhunters are truly smart? Aggressive, canny, cunning, dedicated...tough, to be sure, but smart? I have often been given cause to wonder. Certainly, approaching the steep, slick trail on boots with soles that possessed the contour of a surfboard may have been macho, each step an aggressive approach to my cunning plan of a craftily placed tree stand, but smart? Not!

With the pack dangling from my right elbow, which did nothing to improve my balance, I pressed on. What is it about the promise, perhaps hint is a better word, of a chance encounter with that buck of our dreams that pulls us into such wretched circumstance and conditions? "Like Lancelot, I suppose, in his quest for The Holy Grail," I had mused as I slipped downward.

The stand was in the next drainage: a long line of mixed cedar, hackberry, Bois d' Arc, persimmon and assorted oak that meandered for miles north from the Caney River connecting large stands of timber with its wandering thread. It was a corridor, a travel route punctuated with rubs and scrapes, pockmarked with telltale tracks and droppings. There were rubs on 10-inch cedars; spindly sumac and the tattered willows that bordered the old pond dam in the middle had been beat to a frazzle. Green winter grass had sprung under Bois d' Arc whose heavy, yellow horse apples lay scattered, their texture and shape suggesting the disposable brains of alien invaders. Some showed signs that the deer were beginning to use them. Many lay in ruined, chartreuse piles where the fox squirrels had shredded them in systematic attack.

It was a place you could believe in. The stand was on the south side where the timber had thinned and spread, offering a full field of clear fire across its 30-yard width. To the left, three main trails merged, and while deer could pass through anywhere, odds were a shot would be at the junction 19 yards away. It was 6:35 a.m. when I reached the tree. The gray morning turned quickly to light silver as the wind roared down the draw whipping the taller trees into a thrashing dance, their naked branches like stretching black tentacles grasping at the sky.

In my mind—the part that thinks it's smarter than a deer—I thought the deer would be bedded down. But I learned long ago that the high winds in Kansas and those to the south of where I live in Oklahoma are no barrier to the movement of prairie deer. "The best time to go is when you can," I had thought. Although I was miserable from the penetrating cold, I had been there to make the most of it. In the tree, safely belted on the swaying platform and glad of it, I noted a fresh rub to my right. The bucks were hot, giddy with testosterone overload. "I think something will happen," I had whispered to myself. "Two hours, I can hang on for two hours." Two more heat pacs were popped, those miracle dry-chemical things that heat quickly even in the cutting cold. One wrapper whipped from my grasp sailing downwind, a bright-orange beacon that disappeared into a tangle of fallen leaves.

For a surprisingly long while I had been comfortable. The tree swayed in roundabout oscillations. Bundled, I cuddled myself, with my hands in the warm chest pockets. The guys that designed this had been cold before. I make a mental note to drop them a line: Dear Sleeping Indian Guys, I think you have been cold, too!

Soon though, the cold started to reach inside. I thought about my layered winter wear and decided I'd done all I could. I have never found anything that keeps my feet warm! I peeked at my watch: 7:10 a.m. Twenty-five minutes, was that all? I hate cold-weather bowhunting. Why am I doing this? Because you have to. Why? Because it's what you do. Because you seek The Grail. Because, deep inside, you really do love it.

Thirty minutes later I spotted a flicker of movement. A doe had been in the trail. How did she get this close? I should have seen her coming. She had been goosy, uncertain. She couldn't smell me; she didn't see me. It's the wind. She trotted on. Will there be a trailing buck? I eased into a better ready position, keyed up like a hunting hawk searching for a mouse. The buck came. Sleek and fine, but only a tweaker six-point rack, not why you hunt in Kansas. At 8:30 a.m. a doe and fawn fed by. The doe constantly snapped up her head.

Nothing followed. At 8:50 I decided to give it 10 more minutes.

The woods were filled with sound. The last leaves rattled clinging to their tenuous, weakening grip. Branches clattered, large limbs squeaked and groaned protesting the punishing wind. I can't hear well. I hate that. Movement off the right quarter. I leaned forward to peer into the tangled bottom. A leg moved, the flash of an ivory antler. Good buck!

He moved away. He must have come from the north and he'd circled. I fumbled for the grunt call. It was futile. If he heard it, which I doubt, he didn't care. He's following the trail of the doe and fawn. Damn! I shook hard. Sure, seeing the buck might have triggered it, but the cold had pushed deep beneath my layers. Not good. It was time to leave. I hated to, but I was finished. Staying was not smart.

To my left, down the creek, a fox squirrel let loose a hysterical run of chirring barks. They often do that when a deer passes. It was thick down there. The squirrel chattered again. My trembling had eased a bit. The bow hung loaded with its sleek, ice-cold missile. I wondered if I could pull it. I shrugged my shoulders rapidly under the wool parka, which helped a little. I leaned forward to watch downstream. I'd give it 10 more minutes.   ▲

Deep
Freezes

Excuse me if I step on some toes here, but I have never made any bones about it: When it's cold, not chilly, but really cold, I just don't think bowhunting is a lot of fun. Could be it has to do with my Southern California Beach Boy roots? Who knows? But you know what? I will go when it's cold.

I think it has something to do with not going hunting 'cause I want to, but because I have to! I mean, it's not like I'm being forced into it; my wife doesn't order me afield because we need meat. No, there's usually meat in the freezer by now, carefully wrapped testimony to lucky sojourns around the country that started last August. Right now, in fact, there's most of an elk, half a mule deer, two whitetails, about 20 mallards and I think maybe two turkeys left.

Nope, it ain't like we're gonna go hungry. I go hunting because I need to be there; the craving to be bowhunting is greater than my God-given good sense to come in out of the cold.

When I was a young man in California we bowhunted mule

deer from mid-July through January. Southern California weather in December and January is about as intimidating as a newborn kitten; we hardly ever gave it much thought. So I grew up knowing bowhunting as a pastime generally conducted under relatively balmy conditions.

Even when we began to branch out to other states during the major bowhunting month of September—mule deer and elk places like the Kaibab in Arizona, northeastern Nevada, southern Utah, Idaho and Colorado—cold, real cold, was never a factor, though it occasionally snowed lightly and rained frequently.

All of this, of course, was before whitetails crossed my trail and screwed up the balance of my bowhunting life and its perspectives relative to ideal climactic environment. I quickly learned that very cold weather and inhospitable conditions are frequent and integral parts of the game, a point brought abruptly to my attention on my first whitetail hunt.

In the late 1960s Jim Easton and I flew to Michigan to join members of the Archery Manufacturers Organization (AMO) for a meeting and the continuation of a data-collection project that dictated we had to hunt in order to bring it to conclusion. As you might imagine, I considered this the sorrier portion of my job description with the Ben Pearson Company, but accepted the detail magnanimously rather than subject the dismal task to another member of the staff. It was the only honorable thing to do.

At the get-go two observations provided worrisome insights to this whitetail-hunting thing. The first was the view from several miles aloft of Lake Michigan. Those gorgeous emerald waters I had seen often during summer months were now mostly solid. "It must take some hellacious cold weather to freeze something nearly the size of the Pacific Ocean," I mused. The involuntary shivering of dread that seized me gave way to a full-grown hypothermic fit (the second observation) when we deplaned.

Fred Bear met us in at the airport amidst a landscape covered with snow knee-high to a tall giraffe. The wind, out of the north, was blowing hard enough to hold the flag dead stiff (though perhaps it was just frozen that way). Both Jim and I were not heartened by Fred's pronouncement: "There's a storm coming and it might turn cold!" Jeez! With one wool shirt, a sweater and a camo jacket in my bags, I figured we were goners!

During that era, hunting from elevated stands was prohibited in Michigan. I suspect the fact we hunted from ground blinds that offered some protection rather than aloft is what preserved me from becoming a popsicle—that and wearing all the clothes I could borrow. Bob Kelly said I reminded him of his dirty clothes hamper.

Being acclimated to such miserable conditions, of course, was the key; northeastern guys were used to it. Fred thought the whole thing weatherwise was perfectly jolly. "Great whitetail weather, keeps them up moving to feed" was the sage counsel. But it was not his wisdom that killed me; it was how he dressed for battle: a pair of medium long johns, rather lightweight wool pants, his trademark plaid wool shirt, Borsalino hat and a jacket. But what really blew me away was his footwear: lightweight leather boots and one pair of socks! In borrowed felt pacs and two pairs of socks I felt gangrenous frostbite was the inevitable fate of my toes. While I was in near ruin, Bear was invigorated.

I wanted to shoot a whitetail pretty bad and not just for datum; I was mad at them. My suffering moment finally arrived when a nice buck crunched by through the crusty snow. No first place ribbon, no cigar! Bundled and chilled stiff, my trusted Mercury Marauder would not bend to my will. The buck briefly watched my struggle, then bounded away, the first of a thousand vanishing white flags I was yet to see.

Time, relocation to Oklahoma (where weather watching is a primary pastime) and treks to frosty whitetail haunts the breadth of the land have tempered my resolve and thickened my blood. With gear better suited to frigid conditions I can reluctantly, if not cheerfully endure, which I do because something inside still says: I have to. Just because you love something does not mean you have to like it!

Chapter 11

Thoughts On Shooting

Releasin' The String

I t's been seven seasons since I started using a release. Note that I said using, not shooting. In spite of what you might hear, "shooting" a release properly is not as simple as some would have you believe. However, it is correct to say that a release makes shooting a bow and achieving accuracy easier than mastering the proper use of your fingers. For the record, while I use a release effectively, I really don't use it properly.

Why would a lifelong finger shooter of reasonable skill switch to a release?

For me, it all had to do with the evolution of today's bow designs. In simple terms, short, fast, steep string-angle, 60- to 65-percent letoff bows are not engineered with a finger shooter in mind. For sure, some folks can pull it off. Many will drop off one or two fingers once full draw is achieved. This, of course, eliminates the severe "pinch," which can, and usually does, result in a wild, jerky string "pluck" and a wobbly, errant arrow. As a result, the landing zone is frequently known only to God.

I tried the drop-off-the-finger method. For a guy who used three fingers for well over 30 years, there was no way my brain and body could get in sync. The effect was cylinder-bore scatter with only one missile. It didn't work. So, it was time to try a release.

My reasoning was simple. When shooting at targets, the misses—usually severe left or right—were laughable. Missing real critters—or worse, not hitting them where I was looking—is the sort of thing that gives me nightmares. If I wanted to shoot the newer-style bows, which I did, a release was the obvious answer.

As I've indicated, it took a while to develop a comfort zone and a reasonable level of skill. However, within a short period of time I realized that when it came to accuracy, I was shooting better groups than ever before. Oh, there were problems. At the outset my trained brain told my fingers to let go. Letting go of the entire release unit is not effective—it's scary!

A wrist-strap model helped me solve the double-jink-glitch problem my friends found highly entertaining. It came around though, and after a reasonably short period I was able to switch over to a "concho"-style release, which I prefer. There's just something about having the release permanently attached to my wrist that I found disturbingly distracting. Further, after a lot of practice and in-the-field practical application, I feel I can "lock and load" just about as fast as I used to with fingers.

Most important, I can shoot the shorter axle-to-axle bows so common today with confidence in my accuracy. In fact, without trying to sound like those archery hunters who claim they never miss, I seldom do.

While some downgrade the use of a release as too high-tech, too modern, less challenging or, more ridiculously, an unfair advantage, it's safe to say that perhaps as many as 75 percent of today's archers use one of the many styles available. I have also heard that you cannot use a release with a recurve bow. That's just simply not true. You sure can!

Another fallacy: With the shorter bows and a release, you

have to use a sight. This isn't true either. In fact, when I started using one, I was shooting a compound "bare bow": no sights. Just recently I participated in a celebrity shoot up in Michigan with Ted Nugent. Ted's hunting style, which he has certainly proven to be effective, is a high-anchor, short, pretty fast bow, a release and no sight. He's pretty salty!

There is no question that the vast majority of new archers today are fitted with a release when they get into the game. However, I always recommend that everyone learn how to use their fingers, too. There are a jillion horror stories about folks who had the chance of a lifetime and couldn't shoot because they had either lost or dropped their precious metal fingers. Smart guys learn to go both ways, and smart guys always carry a backup.

If you're a sight shooter, be aware that your bow will not shoot in the same place once you switch from a release to fingers. Learn where the different points of impact are, and you will be well prepared for those hunting moments that fall under the tenets of Murphy's Law.

I feel very comfortable hunting with a release. I know I do not "shoot it" correctly—I can't shoot quarter-size multi-arrow groups by "punching" off the shot. But hunting situations often dictate a "quick trigger" to get the job done. My practice groups are plenty tight though, and when it comes right down to it, under hunting conditions one-arrow groups in the right place are all I'm ever going to need. ▲

No
Apologies
For Change

I t seems bowhunting, which began as a rather simplistic
pastime, gets a bit more muddled with each passing season. Equipment has gone through unbelievable changes
since I started shooting in the mid-1950s.

Although the configuration of bows frequently changes
today, improvements were constantly taking place during the
recurve era. Every year we looked forward to new innovations
from companies such as Bear, Pearson, Hoyt and Wing. It was
just as exciting then as it is today—maybe even more so—albeit
certainly less complicated. Everyone wanted a faster, more efficient hunting bow, and just as it is today, the buzzword was
"fast" or "cast" in the vernacular of that era.

I doubt that engineering design and marketing strategies
differed much from today. Certainly during my long tenure
with Ben Pearson Archery we spent countless hours trying to
work up better, more efficient bow designs as raw materials got
better and better. That was a neat time in an industry and
sport that seemed, as I look back, much more relaxed, more

comfortably paced than today.

Now, for most bowhunters, archery has become high-tech, although some longbow and recurve aficionados still apply their skills (and their method involves considerably more shooting wisdom).

Why do I mention this? Well, because I find it interesting, almost amazing, that few bowhunters realize the effectiveness of "traditional equipment", or its significant role in our heritage as archery hunters. Frequently folks stare in sheer disbelief at the mount of my Cape buffalo taken some years ago with a recurve (perhaps because it happened before some of them were born).

In the minds of many of today's arrow launchers, the fact that every game animal on earth has at one time or another probably been felled by an arrow propelled from a recurve or a longbow is difficult to swallow.

To be perfectly frank, I liked the recurve era somewhat better than today's atmosphere. Maybe that's because back in those days there wasn't such a wide range of theories, egos and equipment around to get archers squabbling. This factionalist attitude troubles me. It's so unnecessary, divisive and counterproductive to the well-being of archery and bowhunting.

Oh, sure, 25 years ago some archers always found something to gripe about; hell, I can remember when some screwballs complained about Easton's shafts being too accurate! Nevertheless, it was a peaceful time, maybe because bowhunting seasons were sort of new, and most of us were closely united in our focus for more and better opportunities. Of course, there weren't nearly as many of us "feather merchants" then, just a few hundred thousand nationwide. It's a far cry from the two million or so archers today, of which only about 10-percent are "traditional archers", a term that strikes me as both honorable and appropriate.

I don't shoot a recurve anymore, though I did for years. Without attempting false modesty, I shot one very, very well. I don't shoot the simple stick because it no longer fits my mood or my commitment to constant practice. In addition, the ravages of time and abuse to the shoulder and the elbow make shooting a recurve an unpleasant and, worse, inept and inaccurate effort. To me, efficient accuracy in the field has always been the priority, and while there's no guarantee that everything will go perfectly every time, the comfort zone of a confident mind is one of life's greatest keys to success.

My decision is mine alone based on what works best for me, considering the game I hunt. I am mind-boggled beyond imagination when, as often happens, I am braced by some jerk who lays into me while riding his traditional bandwagon, labeling me as a sellout hired gun for the money-grubbing compound manufacturers. I was once accused of causing some guy's bowhunting problems, and have several times been told how disappointed someone was in my "crossing over".

None of this has caused me to contemplate terminating my happy existence, but it will sometimes generate loss of sleep as I try to decipher the warped brain currents that lead to such lines of reasoning. I just don't get it. Don't misunderstand me, compound shooters also have more than their fair share of hysterical "techies" who spout off inanely.

The attempt to force philosophies is probably our most troublesome human weakness. How any of us bowhunt should be of no concern to others, if it's done honestly and in good taste. There is neither room nor need in the bowhunting fraternity for petty squabbling. Caught between a deep-rooted love for graceful recurve bows I no longer choose to use, and the compound with which I feel comfortable, provides me with the simplest of views. Bowhunt for your own reasons. And do it in your own way.   ⚊

Trial
And
Arrows

I confess to being a bit laid-back when it comes to my bowhunting equipment. I've always felt that that old adage, "Keep it simple, stupid!" fit me perfectly. Maybe it's a holdover from many years toting a recurve bow; not much is simpler or sweeter than a recurve, well, maybe a longbow. I never could shoot a longbow, but I could shoot a recurve.

Maybe my attitude is based partly on my long-held belief that Murphy's Law was written for archery hunters. Lord knows, I've seen just about everything that could go wrong actually go wrong.

In the good old days, not much went wrong with a recurve. A broken string—usually an accidental cut—was the most common in-the-field disaster; bad deal if you didn't have a spare. I always had an extra one taped to my lower limb.

As a general rule, if a recurve or longbow had a flaw, it showed up in the first 100 shots or so. I have recurves to this day, some of them 30 years old, that are still sound and reliable. I carried a Mercury Marauder by Ben Pearson for the better part of 10 years, shot thousands of arrows from it and took much game while abusing it, oftentimes severely, in the process.

Yep, the recurve was a simpler tool compared with today's well-engineered compound bow. Nevertheless, the lessons I've learned afield with a recurve save me a lot of headaches today when it's time to set up my modern hunting bow for exactly the same purpose: bowhunting.

I suppose some might find this a rather plain perspective, but in my opinion, the only purpose the bow serves is to deliver the broadhead effectively with a minimum amount of confusion, clutter or clatter. My method of setting up a hunting bow for pursuing whitetails: I use the same equipment for everything. It's my theory that the fewer parts and pieces involved, the fewer parts and pieces to worry about. I've seen some pretty serious hunts ruined for lack of a replacement screw, an extra spring or intricate little crandoodle that made the zigomite activate the whatchamacallit. To each his own. I've sat in camps where folks couldn't keep from fiddling with the working parts of their bows and rests, equipment that should have been in perfect function when it arrived. We call them "Allen wrench addicts".

I select a bow for its feel. I suppose we all do that. I like one light and do everything I can to keep it that way. I've never recognized a need for a stabilizer on a hunting bow, though it can help reduce bow noise. I just don't want the extra weight. If the string is served with monofilament I remove it and re-serve with braided Fast Flight. It wears better—never worn one out—and it's quieter when shot with a release.

Then I glue thin, soft leather to the inside of the sight window from four inches above the rest down and around to the outside edge of the shelf. This eliminates game-alarming clicks or clinks should the arrow tap against the riser or fall off the rest at the wrong time. Trust me, it happens, and you know what? Whitetails know what it means. If the bow has a removable grip, it's best to line it with double-back tape or a thin coat of silicone. You would be amazed at the amount of noise a loose or hollow grip will generate. As you can tell, I'm very serious about being quiet. I make sure that every screw is firm. I help them stay that way with a touch of rosin.

Next, the cable guard. When damp, or with a slightly worn slide or glide, it can produce squeaks that will send a whitetail into geophysical orbit. I cover mine with very thin Teflon tape and make sure the slide friction points are smooth. Not only is it an aid in reducing bad vibes, but it also makes the bow smoother, easier to draw. I recall a trip to Mississippi last year along with bowhunting author Dwight Schuh. He had his cable guard set up the same way, first time I'd seen anyone else do it. "Great minds," he said. It pays off.

Remember, I'm into simple. I set all my bows up with an N.A.P. Center Rest. I shoot feathers; if you prefer vanes, the Center Rest Flipper is a great choice. Each rest comes with adhesive-backed strips of soft material for the pressure point of the rest. It eliminates the vast assortment of unwanted sounds that occur when you try to draw on the buck of your dreams.

For the string I prefer the acrylic yarn puffs. Properly wrapped into the string, they stay in place and are excellent silencers. Some folks complain about them picking up burrs and such, which they do. But they quiet that bow down far better than anything else.

Anything that mounts on the bow, sight or bow quiver, for example, is shimmed with thin rubber, anywhere there's hard contact. It eliminates noise and makes for a solid foundation.

Sight selection is based on weight and durability. I've seen more damage to sights in the field than any other piece of equipment. Three fiber-optic TruGlow pins have really been a boon for aging eyes, and boy, does that gold one look good tucked tight behind a shoulder.

Finally, I should mention that hardcam bows can be difficult to control under many hunting conditions. Take letting down, for example. Oftentimes letting an arrow down through the severe draw cycle of a hardcam bow will cause a misnock. Not good. A case in point: Last December I was in a tight stand situated very low in a stubby live oak. The buck I wanted came in fast running a doe. The doe passed at 10 yards, and I drew on the buck, who stopped—at seven yards—with only his head and neck exposed. At full draw I waited and waited and waited, and finally I had to back off. I was able to let down easily, without any bump over the gentle Command Cam. I was able to redraw smoothly, with the buck almost in my pocket. How did it work out? I'm pretty good at six yards.

Simple setup, nothing fancy. Just one guy's way of doing it. But you know, I haven't had a run-in with Murphy in years. ▲

First
Impressions

I think it has something to do with the fact that I shot a recurve bow instinctively for years and years, or should I say barebow, or simply a recurve bow without sights (seeing as how there's allegedly a significant difference between instinctive and barebow).

Well anyway, interpretations of style aside, I always thought in terms of yards. I'd study the target zone as I prepared to shoot and thought about it in increments of yards: 25, 30, 35. The point is, in more than 30 years of doing it, I got to be pretty doggone good at estimating yardage. So, when I switched over to a compound and sight, which demands accurate yardage calculations, it was really kind of a piece of cake. It fit my style of working out a shot, and I found, in most cases, that my first impressions of distance and angles affecting the trajectory, i.e. where to hold with a three- or four-position fixed-pin setup, were usually right in the ballpark. With the sight, I was refining my estimations to a finer degree, thinking 33 instead of 35.

Do not misunderstand. I am not suggesting that I never missed, but my misses, and they are many and memorable, most often stem from poor technique on my part or mysterious intervention from the Red Gods who rejoice in cluttering selected arrow flight paths with unseen impediments of assorted flora. Faulty distance calculation was an infrequent culprit.

So, now let me take you to southeastern Kansas in the season just passed.

The campaign in the 1996 Kansas season revolved around the delicate format of filming a whitetail bowhunting video. For those of you lusting to become Technicolor Bowhunting Stars, I offer the following advice: Consider (read, believe) that you are every bit as experienced and handsome as the guy on tape and proceed with your own very precious hunting time uncluttered with the assorted trappings and headaches of filmmaking. Let them provide you the vicarious entertainment through the doldrums of the the dull off-season. You will be much happier, unquestionably better off, and your chances of success multiplied by a factor of five, to the tenth power! Trust me.

Filming (videotaping) is tedious, sometimes back-breaking, most often frustrating, difficult work. Picture the right buck in a perfect place for a shot that the camera cannot cover. You have him dead to rights and are obliged to let him walk. Letting big bucks walk is not my idea of the perfect hunting experience. For these and a myriad of other reasons, mostly selfish, I have studiously avoided involvement in filming projects for more than the last decade. At my age, life is too short, I've had my starring roles and much prefer the solitude of the woods alone with my thoughts unwilling to share them with the peering lens of a $30,000 camcorder. But I did.

It was my affinity for Brad Harris and the gang at Lohman who produce some of the world's finest game calls, and a library of outstanding hunting videos, that caused me to capitulate. They are old friends. I enjoy their company, and accepting the invitation to participate as "expert talent" on some prime Kansas real estate seemed, after some short deliberation, a pretty good choice.

Typical fall weather of the Great Plains rocked and rolled, as it is inclined to do—from sweet frosty mornings and pleasant sun-dappled afternoons to screeching north winds that punctured and probed with clawing, icy fingers. Chances came, almost, then passed, fleeting footage of good bucks that were never quite in the right place. Then, on the loveliest of fall afternoons with a gentle southerly breeze, it all came together.

He was a stunning, nontypical 12 pointer, not quite to his prime in terms of years—$3^1/_2$ years, probably. A handful of does and fawns were contentedly feeding before us when he trotted in, head held low, grunting in lust-induced frenzy. For a time the scampering race through the surrounding oaks as he pursued a matriarch doe seemed destined to take him out of the equation, then it was suddenly over and he was back, walking straight on to center stage.

Full draw was automatic. He was turning, now entering full broadside, and my brain clicked, sending the signal from command central to the steadying, brilliant gold of the fiber-optic pin: 34 yards! I knew the camera was rolling, and I had him in this most perfect of spots, fully framed, zooming in for the crystal-clear close up. He stopped, as though he had read and memorized the script, obliging us as he bent his head to scent the lady deer perfume wafting in the dried brown grass.

Command central changed its signal: 30, 30, 30! The pin lowered, tight behind the shoulder, lower third of the sweet spot, insurance against bolting reaction. Thuumm—missile away!

First impressions born of experience are invariably correct. Deviations are serious transgressions. Mine forever captured on a piece of tape displays with remarkable clarity the folly of change, full frame, sharp as a tack, the flashing XX75 zipping below the snow white belly. While my sin is admittedly painful (stupid?) I am afforded the unusual opportunity of being able to review it at any time. This is something I have chosen not to do. Penance should be a thing of the mind.　　　　**A**

Chapter 12

Bowhunting Musts

The
Proper
Patience

I don't know how many hours I perched in trees last season waiting on whitetails. On one memorably miserable day, I sat for seven hours in all kinds of rain: light rain, heavy drizzle, steady downpour carried on a howling cold north wind. I probably couldn't have shot an arrow if I'd tried—I was doggone cold and uncomfortable. But I had plenty of chances. Eight bucks came by me that day, one bird-dogging, nose-to-the-ground grunting critter after another. I figure a cruiser came by about every 45 minutes. The boys were doing some serious looking. Each time when I said to myself, "This is stupid!" along came another.

It just goes to show that weather doesn't matter much when bucks are hot—and they were hot, mentally and physically. On two occasions I saw steam rolling up off of the bucks' backs in the thickets before they broke into view. It was like watching for an old locomotive chugging up over a distant hill. I was honestly relieved that none of them merited serious consideration, though one was a pretty good 10 pointer, and would have scored close to 125. I figured if I shot him—though I doubted I could have functioned well enough to do it—he would score 124. If anyone else shot him, naturally he would be bigger.

Of course, there were many shorter hunts, the usual morning or evening "posts", as my old friend Len Cardinale calls them. In my part of the country they're called morning or evening "hunts". But "posting" or "standing" may be more appropriate. One guy I know calls them "sits", as in "you get two sits a day". I guess to me, just sitting around poised to strike has never seemed like real hunting, like spot-and-stalk tactics for mule deer or elk do. Strange, though. I don't feel that way about sitting under a shady tree on a hot September day waiting for a zigzagging dove, or scrunching for hours in a December cornfield hoping the mallards will come. Maybe I'm just confused.

The seven-hour stint in the rain was sort of a "sticktoitiveness" thing—one of those days when, if you're there at the right time and place, fate might finally throw you a big buck bone. I was pretty pleased with my dedication—dogged persistence might be a better way to put it. I kept thinking the weather couldn't get any worse, which it didn't, but it didn't get any better. I stuck it out until just about dark, when it was raining so hard I couldn't see 15 feet in front of me.

I have become more patient when it comes to stand-hunting, or even hunting from ground blinds for that matter. There was a time when anything more than a couple of hours became excruciatingly boring. I never get in a stand without a fully charged sense of anticipation. I never walk to one in the predawn darkness without cringing at the noise I think I'm making, even when I know it probably doesn't matter. At those times I stay alert and fully pumped for a longer period of time. Maybe it's because I'm now less impatient with stands that I've learned more about when, where and how to hunt them—even though my big-buck results haven't improved that dramatically. But it's probably because I'm older and have discovered an overlooked streak of patience.

Still, after a few hours, especially during the warmer early-season mornings, I start to fidget. The days are nice and the waters are still warm, so I get to thinking about bass and big bluegill on flyrod bugs. I'm as dedicated a whitetail archery hunter as anyone, but my outdoor interests are varied. Some might think my attitude is flawed. Perhaps so, but it's mine, and I'm stuck with it. It is not so bad on afternoon hunts—ummmm, I mean posts. By fidget time it's dark, and the last 45 minutes of daylight should keep even the least patient person on full-scale alert. I do much better in the afternoons.

Being impatient has cost me, as I suspect it has us all at one time or another. I'm sure there were many times when I left too early, and just as many when I stayed too late. I guess it all averages out; I'll just never know.

I came within a heartbeat of leaving too early one morning last fall. The signs of the rut were slipping into high gear. My preferred afternoon hunting spot was a line of scraggly new rubs in the area. The wind was wrong for my favorite morning spot, but it was good for the other, so I switched. It was a nice, light breezy sunny morning with a hint of fall. The weather had been unseasonably warm, so the touch of a chill was almost welcome. The breeze kept the drying oak leaves clattering enough to provide cover for any little noises I made. I like mornings like that. You can have all those crisp, clean, very, very still mornings some folks just swoon over. All the whitetails I've met hear too well.

I vowed to stay until 9:30 a.m., an hour longer than I figured would be necessary. Morning movement usually occurs very early in this area, but given the increased buck sign leading to the bedding area, a little extra time felt right. At 9:30 I stood up carefully, looked around very carefully (I thought) for one last time and started to lower my bow. The buck stood 25 yards away in the center of my rub-line clearing—right in the middle of the widest, most open part, right where I had just looked. Darn it if whitetails don't have a way of making you feel stupid!

Clattering leaves covered my anxious attempts at reorganization. The buck stood stone-still, staring off to my right. I got my act together, took a deep breath and shot him perfectly. I was watching him go down inside 30 yards when a better buck bolted from the right, just about underneath me. I don't know if I really won that round or not. Let's call it a draw.

All in all, I felt okay about it. Heck, the other buck wasn't really that much bigger. I was pleased with my patience and performance, though admittedly I had pushed the edge of the envelope. Better yet, I didn't have to drag him out in the rain.

You don't really need to know how many hours or days you total up sitting on stand. All that matters is that the job gets done. And when it comes time to figure the score, a draw ain't all that bad. ▲

Just Passing Time

This is the time of year—recuperating from turkey chas'n and awaiting fall expeditions (that really starts in late summer)—when I reorganize. To be honest, I haven't played with my bow and arrow much lately. There were some days when, if things seemed right, I carried my bow on a turkey hunt, and more days when I carried my heavy, time-worn, three-inch, 12 gauge Model 12 Winchester, the old one with a four-digit serial number.

Somehow, when springtime begins to assert itself as a prelude to summer, I find myself at a crossroad in commitment. Looking back, I seriously carried a bow since August of last year through January of this year. I spent many pre-work hours shooting practice arrows in hopes of being physically and mentally ready for a few milliseconds of real shooting action. I am not complaining. It's what I do, but once in a while, especially when the gobblers are getting with it, I think switching gears is a good thing.

As it always does, this bit of springtime side-slipping passes. While some might look at this as a serious character flaw, my thoughts are not yet wholly occupied with the coming bow season. It is not out of my mind, for now, just not at the forefront. For the next month or so, I will spend a great deal of my free time fishing. By actual count, I have more shotguns than fly rods, but more fishing rods in the aggregate than shotguns.

My wife thinks the arsenal is over-abundant—which it probably is—even though I have tried for years to explain the necessity of maintaining every gauge in a variety of styles. She is mollified by the explanation that they are part of the legacy I will leave to our grandsons. It's a good ploy. Grandmothers never think there is enough you can do for grandchildren, and she is exactly right about that.

I do not keep much of a collection of bows, current ones at least. I do have some neat old-timers that I treasure for what they are, or who gave them to me. As for the more recent editions, it seems that every year there's a new Hoyt to wring out that will become the tool of choice for the coming season's campaigns. Sometimes I keep one of the older models, although I usually give them to someone, preferably a youngster it happens to fit.

Around May the sabbatical ends. I'm not sure what causes it, but something triggers my need to start shooting. On an especially good year it might be caused by the abundance of squirrels. I'll see lots of them while seeking out bluegill beds with a two-weight rod and rubber-legged bugs manufactured on winter nights.

The next time I go fishing, a bow goes in the boat along with a handful of arrows, dinged up, hard-used old ones that I'm not concerned about losing, which is their inevitable fate. There will be a battered Zebco 808 attached to the bow and a fish arrow or two. The gar and carp will be in the shallows, and maybe I'll run across a big drum. They aren't too bad on the table, not so good as bluegill, but much better than a common carp.

The squirrels offer tricky, tempting targets. The fox squirrels give you a pretty good chance, the little grays are never still, and never there when an arrow arrives. It's challenging shooting—good practice that starts my arrow-flinging juices flowing. Once in a while I get lucky. I remember the day I picked a foxy out of a towering sycamore. It was an honest 30 yards if it was a foot. There was a pair of guys sitting on a crappie hole bobber fishing minnows about 50 yards away. One yelled aloud, "Did you see what that guy just did?" Minutes later, as my son and I drifted by them, I nailed another running along the bank at about 20 yards. "I can't do that with my .22!" exclaimed one guy. My son said, "Get a bow, it's easy!" I didn't hit another all day, but they weren't around to witness the truth.

By the time the bluegill and big, green sunfish are off the beds my attention is shifting to thoughts of late August and September. The phone lines are busy making plans with friends spread from Michigan to California. Antelope, elk and mule deer are on the early agenda. My wife rolls her green eyes and asks just when I plan on being home. The squirrel-plinking and casual stump-shooting have about decimated my arrow supply. It's time to unwrap a new bundle of XX75s and load up the fletching jigs. I like to make arrows. I get a little fancy with the fletching on the ones I will hunt with; the practice group will be pretty much plain vanilla.

Some of the rods and reels, not all, will get put up pretty soon. My compact travel rods fit in my bow case, an assortment of flies, lure and reels fit in the duffel bag that goes on top of the ever-mounting pile of necessities. I have found there are fish of some sort most everywhere I hunt, and have concluded that there are some things you should never leave home without.

I'll spend the following months doing a lot of shooting. Maybe some new bow will show up to play with, though I rather hope not. I'd like to establish a deeper relationship with the twin set I use right now. And sometime soon letters of confirmation or denial on my hunt applications will arrive. Thinking about them pumps me up. I'm getting that feeling again. Can't you tell?

Getting Ready

Things seem a bit out of sync—but maybe not. I'm sitting here in my office and storage room, the one with all the really good stuff I don't dare to leave in the garage. You know, like binoculars, cameras, shotguns, the best fishing rods, my new Eagle Globalmap GPS, my favorite bows. There's a few glassy-eyed critters staring sightlessly as I ponder: a white-fronted goose I shot at least 35 years ago; a 24-pound Rio Grande gobbler, which, if you don't know, is a helluva Rio; an assortment of African birds and a pretty nice rainbow trout from Idaho. There's just a bunch of stuff.

So, why do things seem out of sync? Well, it's September—almost—two days until the first, a day my family refers to as New Year's Day! That's when summer ends and the hunting season (with doves) starts, when fall really begins. That means it's only four more days before I head for Colorado to chase elk and mule deer with my outfitter and amigo Jay Verzuh. Four more days before the serious fall campaigns begin, and here I sit, working on a column slated for the March issue of next year. Yep, it seems out of sync.

It's my wife Sue's perspective that the room is a mess! I counter with the notion that it is simply cluttered, comfortably so, and that I know where everything is, which removes it from the mess equation. You cannot find things in a mess. I can find everything that I know is in the room, no matter how long it takes.

For a week now there has been an ever-increasing pile accumulating in the middle of the floor, which has significantly reduced the amount of floor space. The pile consists of mostly clothes. It's actually a selection of what's necessary and what's not; and I know I'll probably pack more than I need.

I have one and a half closets full of hunting clothes, mostly camo, and probably a little bit of everything: Advantage, Trebark, Trailcover by Trebark, Mossy Oak, Skyline, Sticks 'N' Limbs, Predator, snow camo. You name it, I've got some, and I'm really quite proud of the collection. Light weight, heavy weight, insulated, waterproof, T-shirts, sweaters, overalls, coveralls, two-piece suits. I even have three pairs of camouflage socks. I have no idea where they came from, maybe someone's idea of the perfect Christmas gift.

The gear I'm gathering up goes in piles according to my checklist, which is broken down into departments. The piles are scattered throughout the house, the bedroom, the garage and my room. The pile on the window seat in the bedroom strikes a nerve, of course, mostly because Sue knows there will be a pile on the window seat in the bedroom until sometime next year. When her eyebrow arches too high, I remind her she signed on for better or for worse: a broad commitment that included cluttered window seats.

Getting ready, gathering up all my gear gets me pumped. I think it's fun, an opportunity to sort through all my toys and treasures, to decide which ones are necessary, to wonder what I did with those 100-grain Judo points. I found them in a film canister marked "100-grain Judo".

Elk hunting requires some slightly different preparation—a bigger knife and sharpening steel, a compact bone saw. I always put lots more nylon rope on the pile than I'd ever need deer hunting. The pile of heavy-duty stuff is the one in the garage: two API Strad-A-Pod tree stands, two sets of Quik Stik ladders, a bag of steps, a bow saw, a tackle box with all the little things a guy might need a long ways from the nearest archery shop. Since I started using a release on the shorter axle-to-axle compounds, I make sure to pack a couple extras.

By the time I get everything sorted and packed, it's pretty compact. The selections from the room and the window seat fit into one duffel bag, including two pairs of boots, binoculars and my four-piece five-weight Sage fly rod, reel with two spools and a fly box. It's a pretty big duffel bag! Yesterday I finished fine-tuning my XX75s with broadheads, Thunderhead 100s. There was one that kept hitting a little right so I culled it and put new blades into the ones that shot to my liking, waterproofed my feathers with Fletch-Dri (great stuff) and packed them in the arrow box. The bows shoot better than I do, an Enticer FastFlite and a new one I can't tell you about now, but by the time this hits the streets you will have heard of it.

I've got a handful of whitetail hunts lined up for this fall. Kansas, Iowa, Texas, Mississippi come to mind, and of course, Oklahoma. Autumn colors, falling leaves rattling in the breeze, hardwood ridges and mysterious creek bottoms are all on the agenda. Sure, I'm looking forward to that. Somewhere a really big whitetail might have my name on it. Maybe I'll meet him this fall. But you know, that doesn't pull at me like elk and mule deer do.

So, maybe thinking about it all now for next March isn't so much out of sync. By then it will be on the front burner again. It will be time to think a bit about September and elk tag applications. Maybe next March I can tell you a story about a big bull, maybe a big buck, too. Maybe, maybe... ▲

Lucky Things

A nticipation is one of life's greatest pleasures. Anticipating the hunting season or a very special trip you have saved and dreamed of for a very long time is essential to a happy outlook. With something exciting on the horizon you can live with your wife's pronouncement that the garbage disposal just backed up.

Second to the anticipating is the planning, and a key part of the planning is the selection of things to bring.

Because certain items are the most important of my important things, considering them in my planning as I gather up my gear is serious business. These things are essential to my hunting trips because they are my Good Luck Things. Take for instance the belt and buckle. I never go bowhunting without that belt and buckle.

Certainly the belt plays an important role because it serves to hold up my pants, and the buckle holds it in place. I have had the belt now for well over 25 years. Brand-new, as a gift, it was a very pretty belt, hand painted with an intricate Indian design, but, alas, time has worn it to near invisibility. It is made of very fine leather, 1½ inches wide and quite thick.

The buckle is an object unto itself. While one day the belt might wear out, which would sadly call for a replacement, the buckle never will. It is a casting in brass with the replica of a bighorn sheep in relief on its oval shape. I have not had the buckle as long as the belt, just 15 years. It was crafted by Marvin Clyncke of Boulder, Colorado, who, in my opinion, besides being a fine artistic craftsman is one of the best archery hunters on planet Earth, and a very good friend to boot. It has my name on the back. Since receiving it as a gift in 1982, I have worn it religiously while bowhunting, considering it a strong totem of good fortune. Being non-superstitious has limits.

The belt further serves to hold a medium-sized knife in its sheath. I do not collect knives. However, as a non-collector, I have garnered one helluva enormous collection of custom blades.

The knife in the sheath is one presented to me many years back. I honestly, and apologetically, cannot recall where it came from. Like good bows, fine guns, whiskey and women, knives are a serious matter of masculine disposition. This particular knife fits mine, and it's packed for every trip. It rides on the belt on my right hip while dozens of its brethren, fine pieces all, remain idle, ignored, unused, at home. It has nothing to do with superstition, it's just my Lucky Knife.

I have friends with severe affinities for certain shirts or jackets, which I find very understandable, because I have a red T-shirt. This shirt is fully 33 years old and looks every day of it. Imagine a tattered rag you might select to wipe off the dashboard of your pickup and you have the picture.

This shirt, except on the rarest of last-ditch efforts in a big game crusade, does not get worn. It contains more holes than O.J.'s defense. My wife, who is fully aware, and magnificently tolerant of my idiosyncrasies, considers saving this my ultimate peculiarity. This shirt, however, adorned my body on occasions (mostly years ago) when I collected many of my finest trophies. Bear in mind, though, that it was worn as an undergarment, I am not now, and never have been, in the habit of stalking big game in a red T-shirt. As a matter of ritual, the shirt (what's left of it) gets packed.

There is nothing superstitious about taking an old friend, which just happens to be a shirt, along with you on a hunting trip.

There are, of course, some things to which we all pay homage and reverent attention, that no matter what our persuasion might be in terms of superstition, are critical. The foremost, of course, is hats. But, the subject of hats is so involved, and at such a level of importance, as to demand serious discussion at length, but, at another time.

Nope. What we are going to talk about is a rock. Quite a few years ago while bowhunting deer, elk and what have you in the state of Montana, I happened to catch a very nice bull trout during a midday lull. A "bull trout", if you do not happen to know, is a lake trout, or mackinaw trout, depending on latitude or local interpretation or on which side of the Continental Divide it happens to strike your lure. Not only did I quite skillfully bring this one to hand, I also prepared it for dinner. Imagine my surprise when, while removing its insides and checking them (which serious anglers often do in order to ascertain whether or not fluttering gold spoons, hammer finished, make up a large portion of their diet), I found within its interior a stone, pear-shaped, half-dollar sized and red ocher in color, and just as silky-smooth in texture as my granddaughter Megan's cheeks. I put the stone in my pocket and we ate the trout. The next day I shot a very large black bear.

Once again I disclaim any strong observance of superstition and no inclination toward the occult. Simply put, I find and pack my stuff for another adventure secure in the knowledge that things should work out. Isn't it really just up to me? Does the fact that the rock has accompanied me afield since its resurrection from the stomach of a trout make it a fetish? Maybe, I'm not sure. I just know certain rocks, like old T-shirts, knives, belts and buckles, are pretty handy things to keep around. ♠

Sloppy Trails

I like beer. In the hottest part of summer, beer tastes pretty good tickling down my throat after a sweltering day on the water trying to tempt a few deep-water bass to bite. I like canned soft drinks, too, and I'm particularly fond of Gatorade to quench my thirst and bolster my electrolytes. When I'm hunting mule deer and elk in late August through early September I keep a half-frozen plastic bottle in my day pack. I like those wax-coated fruit drink boxes also, the ones you stick the little straw in to suck on while you're glassing a bedded buck on the opposite ridge wondering if there's any way to get to him.

I never carry cans in my day pack, but apparently some folks do. I do carry candy and granola bars, Jolly Rancher hard candy (watermelon and strawberry), those little red boxes of raisins and plastic baggies filled with trail mix for a handful of energy. Those are the sort of munchies I stick in my day pack. If I'm going to be out all day I'll probably carry a sandwich sealed in a Ziplock bag, too. By the time I get around to digging it out for lunch it will be flatter than a tortilla, but it still tastes pretty good!

I have decided that when it comes to things I carry in my pack, I'm in the loop, in synch with some outdoorsmen, though not those I care to meet. Why? Because I find their sign, positive proof of it everywhere I go, and I'm really getting tired of it!

I'm sick of beer cans, candy wrappers, pop cans, plastic bottles, bags, six-pack holders, surveyor's tape, juice cartons and other garbage littering our rolling hills, lonesome mountain ridges and deep canyons in the wake of sloppy people. I'm fed up with dug-out fire rings lined with rocks filled with charred, foil-wrapped, scorched garbage in abandoned camps. I wonder: If someone can dig a hole for a fire ring and can't fill it to bury degradable trash, why can't he pack out the rest?

I also wonder: Why can't someone pick up broken glass in a campsite where someone might want to walk bare-footed? I'm nauseated by clear-cuts littered with the dregs of lumbering activity: ruined tires, rusted oil drums, scattered chain saw lubricant containers and abandoned grease-stained overalls. I would like, for just one day, to wander wherever my instinct directed and not find a single can, candy wrapper or plastic evidence left by some jerk who happened to be lucky enough to be there first. I like to go places and fantasize I was there first. There were days and places long ago when I could, but not anymore.

Now the days are like one last season when I trailed a band of elk. I paused that morning beneath a patriarch pine to listen to the cows calling and the bull's occasional bellows and contemplate my next move. At the base of that old tree amid thousands of others in that stretch of rugged Colorado wilderness lay a Beanie Weenie can, a plastic spoon, two granola bar wrappers and three dulled blades from a replaceable-style hunting head. I figured the guy had missed, and it tickled me to death. The wrappers and blades were tucked in a sandwich-sized baggie as though whoever left them wanted to be sure that they would last in their plastic shroud for eternity.

Why do people do that? Do they throw their trash on the lawn at home, or on the living room floor? Not likely. I crunched the can, broke the spoon, stuck them in the baggie and dropped it into my pack. It wasn't so hard to do.

I am amazed at the out-of-the-way places I find the residue of human passage and sloth. It seems almost even odds that any tree I crawl under will shelter a can, most I imagine are beer cans though some are so rusted it's hard to tell. The best place to find cans in the mountains—if you want to go looking for some—is near any body of water bigger than a bird-bath. I wonder: Do people carry full six-pack containers to remote high-mountain lakes for the express purpose of throwing their empties in the water? Seems so, though they can't throw them far enough so they lay there 30 feet offshore glittering in the crystal water until they brown and rot. Maybe they figure the trout like to read the labels. Are not empty cans easier to pack out? To the best of my knowledge, they'd be considerably lighter and much more compact stomped flat. Ah hell, throw 'em in the lake!

Another thing I carry in my pack is a roll of plastic surveyor's tape. I'll use it to flag my way out of a spot where I've left a downed critter in rugged country. Sometimes it's necessary to mark a sketchy blood trail to help establish a line, or maybe to mark a few trees for distance reference from a stand. It's handy stuff, but I don't leave it hanging around. I found a place a few years ago where someone had followed a blood trail with a continuous line of tape; it zig-zagged downhill through a stand of aspen for at least 200 yards. It looked like a crime scene. It was. It's a crime to walk off and leave it. Plastic flagging is easy to gather up and carry out, too, but it seems a lot of people don't.

It seems to me we need to pay closer attention, be more attentive to some of the sloppy things we carelessly do. I don't like to leave anything but my tracks. Neither should any of you.

Chapter 13

My Opinion

The Good
Ol' Days
Are Here

Today it happens more and more frequently as I travel around the country, younger bowhunters asking me questions about the "good ol' days:" What was so and so like? How about the equipment? How much better was the hunting? Sometimes they approach me as if I'm some sort of relic. I suppose that men in their mid-fifties will always look ancient to those in their twenties. The implication doesn't bother me, as tenure does suggest wisdom and experience; it's really kind of neat.

When I was a younger bowhunter, the sport was filled with middle-aged men that were, and still are, our revered legends: Fred Bear, Ben Pearson, Howard Hill and Doug Easton to name a few. The great thing about it was that I got to know them and shoot with them. However, I feel the good ol' days are now, as I will explain.

The dedication to mastering equipment, the degree of difficulty and the commitment involved in using it is easier these days. It's all relative. If you started bowhunting 25 years ago when compounds first appeared on the scene, it was a helluva lot easier than if you had started 30 or 40 years ago learning to master a sleek, handcrafted yew-wood recurve, and English-style longbow or an Osage orange flatbow; or maybe just a tad later with a state-of-the-art, high-tech composite recurve backed and faced with fiberglass; or today, with a compound that's a helluva lot better than the first ones. It all has to do with where you come from.

I've seen most of bowhunting's evolution, from the beginning of the composite stage, mostly, so I can speak from the perspective of a qualified veteran observer.

Bowhunting is easier than it used to be; it's also quite a bit different, which has much to do with it. In the good ol' days, archery seasons were mostly concessions to a minority group that was getting pretty vocal. In the West where I come from, we had limited pre-seasons, usually 10-day, buck-only affairs before gun season started. By comparison to today's bounty, it wasn't much, but we were very grateful for what we got, and it was largely the same throughout the country. Eventually, of course, we got longer seasons, and anytime a season gets longer, success rates naturally get better.

Part of the answer to one of the questions then is: In the good ol' days it was harder because of the limited opportunity and rather primitive equipment! That's the way it was and probably should have been; bowhunters had to prove themselves. I never had a problem with that; we had to prove ourselves, we did, and learned a lot in the process.

Nothing is as hard today as it used to be. High-powered rifles are better, steel shot is better, though I still dislike it, cars and roads are better, arrows are better, optics, medicine, bows, tree stands, communications, fly rods, broadheads, airplanes, level-wind reels, and for the most part, life itself is plainly and simply better. We live and love longer, go to faraway places more easily, spend money faster and, generally, participate directly or indirectly in the ruination of our planet at a break-neck pace. It is man's inherent motivation to plow ever forward as fast as possible. In this Pace Race, I believe nothing has been excluded, even something as serious and old-fashionedly romantic as bowhunting.

Given that, the good ol' days might have been better because of its more relaxed pace; there was a comaraderie then, a bond between bowhunters (maybe all people) that was stronger, probably because smaller groups bond tighter. Bigger groups always seem to accelerate the pace of change and discontent.

In the good ol' days, bowhunters did not shoot very much. The Midwest had very few, if any, whitetails, and it was rare to hear of a deer in Kansas or Iowa; California had a bigger deer herd than Texas! In Michigan, for example, tree-stand hunting was a no-no, the few bowhunters accessible to lots of whitetails had to hunt them from the ground, which has never been easy.

If it wasn't for the whitetail explosion, bowhunting wouldn't be as strong as it is today. You can say the same thing for the equipment's evolution. I will never say that what we have today is better if you want to talk capability in the hands of a competent user; my track record with a simple recurve and that of many of my close friends proved that wrong a long time ago. Actually, what we were proving was the effectiveness of the arrow, but, let's not get into subtleties, getting it in the right place has always been the issue, not what gets it there!

I work with, communicate with and hunt with a good, many people who prefer, in today's vernacular, "traditional equipment." In most cases, they are superb archers within the limits they have established for themselves. In every case, they are exceptional hunters. Some, of course, resent the infusion of today's equipment, it rankles their sense of spiritual values somewhat, an emotion to which they are rightfully entitled, but one in which they wisely keep among themselves. You see, they realize that things change; they also realize that still, today, they have the right and freedom to pursue their thing, their way and so does the other guy. There is something else they realize that has much to do with why the good ol' days are now. We have lots of bowhunters today, many, many more than the good ol' days, and we need them; actually, we need more.

It's really a matter of proportion. Thirty or 40 years ago when fewer of us were beating on our pots and pans to be heard, there weren't nearly as many people to listen, and—check this out—hard-core anti-hunters were in short supply, and animal rights, along with its stupid, new-generation terrorism, hadn't been invented. We live in a different world today, a world where numbers, percentages and dollars dictate everything. Show me someplace that they don't; I want to go there.

I don't think there is any question among those of us involved in the argument for bowhunter's rights that the vision of Glenn St. Charles in developing the concept of the Pope & Young Club was anything short of a monumental notion. It was the major stepping stone on the path to proving bowhunting's worth. The club was founded in those good ol' days; let me provide an example of how things have changed. In 1975, the club published its first edition of Bowhunting Big Game Records of North America. This volume encompasses entries compiled from 1957. In the category of typical whitetail deer, there were 591 entries and 334 black bear. In April of this year, the fourth edition was released, its pages list 8,819 typical whitetails and 2,512 black bear! I've lived and roamed through a large part of the good ol' days, shot my first deer with a bow in 1954, and while I can and do look back on the '50's and '60's with fond recollection of good times and fine people, there's no doubt that what I like to do best is better now than ever. ▲

Outlaws
And
Phonies

S itting around with a bunch of archery hunters relaxing and telling good stories is something I usually enjoy—except for last weekend. This nerd started shooting off his mouth about the sorry state of affairs bowhunting is in, and how it had just totally ruined poor Donald Lewis' life. He claimed if bowhunting wasn't so cutthroat and competitive, good ol' Donnie wouldn't have gotten caught up in all that Yellowstone stuff. He suggested that archery manufacturers are causing all the problems—forcing a guy to do those kind of things so he can make a living!

Is this guy dense, a goon or what? I couldn't believe where he was coming from—like Lewis was some sort of hero that had been unjustly persecuted. Let's get real. Lewis' actions were those of a cold-hearted, calculating, conniving crook. He was prosecuted, not persecuted. In my opinion, he got off too easy.

Yet Lewis contends it was just that which made him do it—a crawfishing, worm-squirming plea that's given the anti-hunters out there another drum to beat for all it's worth. Not only did he do what he did, he tries to sully all the rest of us in the process. Poor ol' Donnie indeed!

What bugs me is how he managed to bamboozle so many intelligent people for so long (including some folks formerly with this publication) with all those made-up mule deer stories. I'm not clairvoyant, but I guarantee you a bunch of us "old-timers" knew it was just a matter of time. Ah well, I've given him more ink than he deserves.

Let's switch gears.

Several years ago, a guy from Idaho set off on the same sort of crooked course. He wrote a book about bowhunting bulls and bucks built around some of the most off-the-wall hunting "secrets" you ever read—all backed up with piles of giant bucks, of course. He received a lot of national exposure as well, including a major feature in one of the Big Books even though the editor at the time, a conscientious kind of guy, was advised that the ointment was full of struggling flies. The big boss overturned the editor's concern—it was a good story—and eureka!

Another hero is born, invented, fashioned, whatever. Well, as we hope will happen to all phonies, eventually he got zapped, first by trying to slip an altered mulie—a huge critter—into the Pope & Young records, then by a few other transgressions that came to light regarding the origin of certain deer or the method of their demise.

Another Bad Boy cheating his way to phony stardom bites the dust. Hooray!

I could spin a few more such yarns. I have a rather high recollection of "bad guys" assimilated over several decades. Most of them committed rather minor offenses—mostly stupid rather than seriously treacherous. Some, I'm sorry to say, really stink. Or I can tell you about current ones going down that promise to create quite a flap. But this is not a gossip rag, and I have no desire to dwell at length on unpleasant subjects. I would, however, like to clear the air about the opinions expressed by the nerd of last weekend. So I'll make a few personal observations.

I take serious exception to the suggestion that manufacturers force folks into foul deeds in order to sell more products or to elevate the image of their chosen spokespersons. I believe it just isn't done. However, like any of us, they can get the wool pulled over their eyes.

Over the years, I have met several men who turned out to be outlaw hunters. Some were bowhunters; some were not. Without exception, they were seemingly all-around great guys. Fun, likable, charming. What they were, though, were con men—the same type that would bilk a little old lady out of her last dime. Crooks! No one knowingly latches onto a crook or a phony except another one, but now and then anyone can be conned.

There are a lot more phonies running around out there than real crooks. I know of several. Beginner phonies are simply liars on their way up, only a step away from "phase two". Once they reach it, it's pretty easy to get tangled up in their ambitious webs and "kerplunk" in their own mess. I believe their warped egos make this inevitable.

Bowhunting is no different than any other walk of life: Every element has its liars, cheaters and phonies. Sometimes boxers take a dive, ballplayers shave points, cadets cheat on exams, clergymen turn out to be perverts, bankers embezzle from their clients and some cops take bribes—let's skip politicians and government.

These are rare transgressions in society's broad spectrum—reminders that it is not a perfect world filled with perfect people. Never has been, never will be. It is naive to think that all bowhunters are straight arrows, and fly fishermen never use bait. Is it equally naive to think that all archery manufacturers are saints? I hope not.

We have to believe in something.

Archery is no different than any other sport—heroes have always been a part of it. Bowhunting is bigger today, which means there's room for more heroes. There is nothing wrong with this. The folks who complain about this are simply jealous wannabes.

The sad part is the suspicion that proven bad guys place on others. Jealousy frequently rears its ugly head when some guy who seems unusually blessed or lucky comes along. The nerds want to take him down; they cannot handle another's success. I've been in this game a long time, even had a little bit of the spotlight. But I've mostly enjoyed a career of mediocre successes.

I remember, though, years ago when I shot a really big moose. At the time it was number three in the records, so it was a pretty good one. A friend of mine called me to say that someone told him I had shot the animal from out of a plane. With my bow!

Pretty tricky, huh?

As bowhunting grows, there will be new heroes and new pretenders. This will never change. There is no cure, though my weekend acquaintance feels that manufacturers should not have contracted spokespeople or shooting staffs. Bowhunting, he claims, is not Nike, Pennzoil, Budweiser or Addidas. He's right, of course—it's Hoyt USA, Bear, PSE, Martin and Easton, to mention a few, excluding the one embroidered on his shirt. I think they would want him to take it off.

No, bowhunting will have its few bad guys, and when they are found out, bowhunting and the law will deal with them. Then, when the sorry scoundrels look in the mirror, their own "Trail's End" will be looking back.　　　▲

Info Exchange

Newcomers to bowhunting whitetails as well as those long on experience are always interested in what the other guy uses, how he does it and why. It's how we learn: Sharing information and our experiences with one another. For the last two years I have spent much of my time participating in bowhunting seminars at major events, such as the Petersen Publishing Company/Ducks Unlimited Great Outdoors Festival, the National Wild Turkey Federation's annual convention, the Illinois Deer & Turkey Expo, Anderson's International Bowhunter's Clinic, to mention a few. I enjoy it—exchanging ideas, strategies, theories and swapping hunting tales.

Having just wrapped up another event tour, I thought it might be interesting to share some of the themes and interesting perspectives I continue to run across all around the country.

Do deer calls really work? What kind—bleats, grunts, rattling? Deer-calling questions are at the forefront of bowhunter interest. They will all work under the right conditions, at the right time. Personally, I believe that they are commonly overused and abused. I see guys carrying grunt calls in early October. I think that's too early and unnatural.

Bleat calls will work early in the season, mostly on does, fawns and yearlings. A good buck could show up but I wouldn't count on it. I have great faith in grunt calls when the rut kicks in. However, hammering on a grunt tube as if you're working a flock of distant mallards isn't my idea of imitating something natural. Nonetheless, there was a fellow in Wisconsin with the ever-present photo album of giant bucks that he claims he collected with what he termed "gregarious grunting", which he insisted on demonstrating. The sounds were harsh and loud, and his face turned an interesting shade of blotchy red. It reminded me of a sick goat. But it must work because he had the photos to prove it and a briefcase full of calls he was hustling.

Sure, rattling works, and there are few things that will give you a bigger adrenaline charge than a buck coming in hard and fast to "the horns". Rattling produces best where there is a high buck-to-doe ratio, although it can work anywhere.

Opinions vary on the size of real antlers. I have a friend that carries a set of mule deer sheds, about a 150-class buck for rattling whitetails. He believes in volume. I carry a set off of a rather unusually palmated eight-point whitetail (probably in the 120s) that seem just right for serious clacking or subtle tickling. If you don't have a set of real antlers, synthetic imitations will do though extreme cold is hard on them.

Tree stand position is one area where opinions vary the most. Of course, it all has to do with cover and wind, wind being the most important consideration. I am quite certain that most of my peers prefer stand positions that are considerably higher than mine, yet I stick to the conviction that the lower, the better. This simply means that I have to find the right spot to place a stand at 10 to 12 feet. Usually I can.

The lower the tree stand, the flatter the shot angle. Flatter angles provide a better avenue for double-lung hits and less arrow interference of muscle and bone for complete penetration, and they are less critical shooting-wise. I don't like the angles from 20- to 30-foot stands and I will admit to being fearful of them, too. I get away with lower stands wherever I can just fine, and I don't have nearly as far to climb—or fall! I set up all my stands to shoot sitting down. If I have done my homework, I know within a radius of 35 to 40 degrees, usually less, where the shot will be. On a stand with a smooth swiveling seat (I prefer API's Strad-A-Pod), I can easily turn silently to cover a field of fire of nearly 300 degrees.

If I cannot draw my bow while sitting down with my bow arm extended horizontally at waist level—with or without bulky clothes, warm or cold—then the draw weight is too heavy. I do not need a 75- to 90-pound compound bow to shoot whitetail deer from a tree stand or at 20 yards. I'm far better served with quiet, controlled bows that spit a razor-sharp arrow into a 10-inch target zone at that range, or farther. I am reminded of the lad, an average-size guy, who approached me in Michigan. His battle plan: an 85-pound Hoyt Defiant matched with Easton's new 2613 and Thunderhead 160s, so he "could knock 'em down".

So armed he could probably knock over a truck. My suggestion that it was a tad unnecessary, explaining that arrows are not designed to "knock 'em down" failed; his mind was made up. In the cold of mid-November somewhere in Michigan his "Big Buck Moment" will come. I predict he will grunt like a bull elephant when he tries to pull 85 pounds, and that his chance for knocking one down is one in 15.

I run into a lot of interesting scent theories. There was a guy who concocted his own blend of cabbage and anise oil along with something else I don't recall for sure, vanilla maybe. He boiled it in the kitchen, this confirmed by the resignedly defeated, affirmative nod of a patient wife. "For better or for worse!" she quipped as they walked off.

There is always lots of good talk about trailing or attractor scents, something I do use and truly believe in. I used to trap gray foxes when I was a kid with sardines as bait in a routine cubbyhole set. Lo and behold, I met a guy who swears that sardine oil on his boots causes bucks to walk right to his tree. "Really!" I said. "You bet!" he replied. He didn't have any pictures though!

I pass on my perspectives, making no claims that my ways are the best ways, just one guy's way that seems to work pretty good. I do get pretty adamant about ethics and behavior, though, and point out that every bowhunter should (in my opinion) belong to his or her state bowhunting organization. And occasionally, an indignant animal-rights extremist infiltrator appears to liven things up. I try to be politely firm in my convictions, admitting they are entitled to theirs. It's not easy, they're really fruitcakes!

The best part is hearing the other guys' ways, looking at their pictures, sharing ideas, mutual brain picking about where and when to go. There's always something new to mull over and think about trying, which reminds me: I wonder where Sue keeps the vanilla? I've got a can of sardines and a cabbage I want to boil. ▲

Opinions

Opinions are personal views and the most common root of argument. The offering of opinions establishes a particular point of view. According to the dictionary (here in excerpt form), an opinion can be submitted as: A) "Belief or conclusion held with confidence but not substantiated by positive knowledge or proof." Or B) "Judgment based on special knowledge and given by an expert."

I'm seldom argumentative on hunting matters anymore, or fishing tackle subjects either, though don't think for a second I can't be. But time has tempered me, that and the realization most opinions are biased perspective, like debates over feather fletching vs. plastic. I have better things to do with the time I have left and prefer to let sleeping dogs lie. Occasionally, however, I'm inclined to express an opinion. For instance, a recent exchange on bear hunting and dogs—let me set the scene.

Picture a major arena housing an outdoor show of considerable size: several hundred displays and 25,000-plus people. I was there as a seminar speaker. Though I'm uncomfortable and not much of a speaker, the invitation to be one suggests I'm an expert; refer to Category B.

Several brother "experts" and myself were watching an extremely good video of a hound hunt for bears in the booth of a northwestern outfitter. The video was also exciting. The bear was huge, ornery and delivered the dogs (three) a serious whackabout thrashing. The outfitter commented on the fact they'd been trailing this bear for a week. "Wouldn't tree," he said. "Been kill'n sheep all summer fer the hell of it. S.O.B. got two of our houn's, good ones too. Yessir boys, 'at's some bear!"

By then there was a fair crowd gathered 'round clogging the aisle as the final scenes played out. The camera zoomed back, revealing a fellow with a bow fully cocked. The fellow with the bow (blue overalls, gray sweatshirt, red baseball cap) waited for the right moment and uncocked it with a snap, whereupon in less time than it takes to recite it, 'ol Bruno—the marauding, sheep kill'n scourge of the West—expired. "Wow!" someone softly exhaled. "Great shot!" "Chicken poop!" a guy next to me snorted. "That's no way to bow hunt!" He was a husky guy in a patch-studded jacket reminiscent of a race car at Daytona. His eyes swept about, noted my embroidered shirt (embroidered shirts with your name under a company logo also support Category B), met mine and inquired, "Whadda you think, Mr. Dougherty, ever hunt bears this way? With dogs?" Oh, hell, I thought. Here we go. "Yes, many times. Cougars, too."

Hunting with dogs is as old as hunting itself, and that's what it is: hunting with dogs. Rifles, pistols or bows are just tools that you carry along, though it's best you know how to use them. I have great admiration for a pack of well-trained hounds, and I have unlimited regard for the men that train and follow them. Without question, they are among the smartest, toughest, experienced outdoorsmen I've ever met. Hunting bears and lions behind dogs is exhausting and often dangerous. It can knock you down on all fours gut-puking sick just trying to stay in the game, yet those that have never done it just smirk and claim it's too easy; that shooting something bayed or treed is unfair (shooting something from a tree is okay) and shouldn't be considered real hunting. Well, I have a problem with that, though of course it's just an opinion, but as long as it's legal and Fair Chase (Fair Chase rules with dogs are explicit) I accord it the respect of real hunting.

The husky guy paused, "Did you like it?" "Yeah!" I replied. "It's interesting, exciting. I liked it a lot." "And you've shot bears that way?" "Yep, and cougars, too." "Well," he went on. "I can't see any challenge or excitement shooting a bear some dogs led you to; doesn't seem ethical!" There was no point trying to explain that the shooting is not the essential element of the hunt; in fact, (another opinion) it's but one piece in a patchwork of parts. Instead, it prompted a question.

"Have you hunted bears?" I asked the fellow. "Yeah, shot three," he replied. "Cool. Whereabouts?" "Canada, in Ontario, we go every spring." "That's great. Hunt with an outfitter?" "Uh, huh, good one, got a great setup." "Bait stations and tree stand I s'pose, right?" "Yeah, they sure work good."

"Okay, so tell me. You go to Canada and hunt with an outfitter, from his stand over the baits he's set up. You sit in the tree with black flies and mosquitoes and shoot a bear that might have his head in a bucket. I know that's exciting, but is it more challenging and ethical than chasing a bear you might never catch through 10 miles of gut-straining mountains? The dogs find a bear, the outfitter finds your stand. Help me out here; I'm having a problem seeing any real difference. I guess you're just against hunt'n with dogs."

"Hell, I love hunt'n dogs. Got three of the best pointers in the state!" "Big running dogs?" I asked. "You bet, and they'll honor and hold a covey 'til hell freezes over." "And you chase after them, find the points, admire their staunchness and straight tails, then wade and flush up the covey?" "You bet, I love it, it's great!"

Me too, it is great. Real hunt'n. Pretty much like chas'n after bears.   ⚘

Last Chance?

I've been thinking about bears lately, which is unusual for me. Normally, I don't pay them much attention anymore unless I stumble over one in Colorado while elk huntin' with Jay Verzuh's outfit where they have become common, even bothersome at times. I haven't hunted a bear since I can't remember, though I admit to seeing two in the last few seasons that had me wishing for a tag. One had an attitude that suggested (having) a tag a moot point. I don't like it when they rise on their hind legs, bow their neck and glare in my direction. Anyway, the thought of bear hunting's been gnawing at me. Among other things, it was triggered by the letter.

It came from a young fellow in Wisconsin I'd met and visited with at one of the big Deer Classics my friend Glenn Helgeland produces. I had responded with sage advice to his questions. Considering that I have sons older than he, and have bowhunted for a very long time, I'm entitled to consider my responses to his questions as wise. After we spoke, as is my way, I gave him my card and told him to feel free to call or write anytime I might be of help; thus, came his letter.

After salutations he explained that he was going spring bear hunting in Ontario and questioned if I would choose an expandable—or mechanical point, as some like to describe them—when shooting a bear. To which I responded: No! I much prefer in-line razor-edged blades behind sharp, penetrating points, particularly on shaggy-haired creatures. My choice, and we'll let it go at that. This is not intended to be a critique or debate on equipment. There are more important issues to discuss. You see, it doesn't matter what hunting head—or bullet—any one of us might choose to use to hunt bears in Ontario, because we can't! Spring bear hunting in Ontario has been stopped!

Did you know that? Some of you might; most don't. Almost every one of you, me too, probably would have said, "Don't worry. They can't (won't) do that!" Well, they did! And just who did? who are they? Was it game managers, researchers, trained professional wildlifers concerned about the (bear) population's well-being who felt there was a problem? No! Are bears in Ontario endangered? No, no problem there! So, who closed the spring season? The Ontario Government—specifically the Ministry of Natural Resources, that's who.

Is there any rational reasoning to this impudent act, this complete disregard for professional, scientific input, public opinion or the debilitating financial impact on that portion of Ontario's population that serves and relies on visiting sportsmen and women, hunters and fishers and tourists for their livelihood? Those who offer lodging, gas, groceries, bait and tackle, food, guide services and friendships?

Is there a rational reason to ignore a majority response of nearly two-to-one in support of the spring season? Sure there is, rolling over to animal rights whackos and anti-hunting zealots whose deep-pocket big bucks are slipped from theirs to anothers is rational as hell. It's just a matter of perspective, and now you know theirs, and why the season is closed.

Spring bear hunters lose, probably just a tip of an iceberg lurking to scuttle all hunting in Ontario, but what of those folks who rely on sports people both foreign (us) and domestic to survive? I have a friend who operates a lodge in Ontario for whom this edict is disastrous. Hunting and fishing is her livelihood, and the fishermen mostly are hunters, too. "Not to worry," suggests the smug Ministry, who in part of a press release implies that they (the Government) will help them in developing new markets and opportunities to get by. Sure, and I can give Jack Nicklaus four strokes a side straight up at Augusta!

"That's Canada for you!" a friend of mine said last night, suggesting, I think, something similar could never happen here. He's wrong; in part, it already has. Look around where our own bear hunting is concerned; spring (and fall) hunts curtailed or drastically reduced. No dogs, no baiting, limited tags, though bears are thriving. Bears are soft, sweet, friendly, cuddly ammunition—along with big money—in today's politically oriented war on hunting.

Think about the anti-hunting initiatives that have appeared on the ballots of November elections; decisions placed in the hands of an increasingly anthropomorphic addicted—bears are cute—doves are sweet birds—no honest clue. Oh, I guess that's not a good thing—society, rather than recommendations of realistic, wildlife management wisdom—though isn't it true that supporters of our anti's agendas now walk heavily in the corridors of our wildlife agencies both as scientists and political appointees? Yep!

Tip of the iceberg poised and waiting to poke another hole here, south of the Maple Leaf border. Yeah, I think it could happen here!

So, I've been thinking about bear hunting a bit harder. This year I can buy a fall bear archery tag over the counter for the area I hunt in Colorado—no limited draw. That suggests to me that reason and wisdom in wildlife management is still here to give me that opportunity. I think I'll take them up on this chance. Lord only knows how long it will last. ♦

Chapter 14

The Important Things

The Important Things In Life

If people are truly lucky in life, they can look back from time to time and count their blessings. These blessings might include a wonderful spouse, fine children, a great hunting dog, a shotgun that points like a finger and a bow that fits one's hands, muscles and spirit.

Admittedly, some may view this order as a subject for debate.

Regardless, the elements are rock-solid, and, in my mind, remain as listed. For me, nothing is more important than my wife and children; I have been married for 36 years and have five children.

I have also been blessed with one great dog. There were other dogs along the trail, one was good enough to remain a pleasant memory, but Triple, a black Labrador, was simply the great-dog bonus of life to which everyone who loves gun dogs should be entitled. Like a beloved wife and great children, he cannot be replaced. After his passing, I decided to get out of the dog business, contenting myself to watch his son under the handling of my own son when time and circumstances allow us to share a duck blind or work a tight patch of pheasant cover.

Regarding the matter of fine shotguns, I'm a bit on the fickle side. My den is cluttered with too many guns, a lifetime of laboring under the assumption that one cannot have enough. That probably isn't true; I have never been able to shoot more than one at a time, though I have had several along on the same trip. The bottom line is simply that I love them and have rationalized their collection as investments. However, if the truth were known, none are of exceptional value, although several have helped me win substantial amounts of money. Ultimately, their fate lies in the hands of my children and grandchildren. In spite of the fact that there are three dozen or so smoothbores in my collection, only one is considered sacred; a battered old Browning. I acquired this treasure in 1957, a week after my marriage, when, between us, my wife and I had to look pretty hard for two nickels to rub together. The fact that she accepted and understood my need for possessions, says volumes in the discussion of blessings and their prioritization.

We have now come to the matter of bows. Considering that archery and bowhunting have played major roles in my life, I imagine that placing bows last on my list might strike some as a bit contradictory.

It all has to do with change.

You see, in the 40-some years that I have been doing the bow-and-arrow thing, archery equipment has changed quite a bit. Shotguns haven't changed very much; a 40-year-old good one still feels and shoots the same. Dogs haven't changed at all; if you get a smart one, everything works out rather well. And, of course, it's not wise to make references to 35 years of social change in women, so we'll let that one go. Bows, though, are different.

Over the years I have acquired several great bows: bows that are simple, perfect extensions of my mind and might; bows in which I had, at the time, the ultimate confidence; bow that today wouldn't permit me to hit the broadside of a barn.

In my den there are three recurves that I hold in near reverent regard. One is a Howard Gamemaster circa 1960, another is a Bear Kodiak TD of the same era, indelibly autographed by Fred; both have seen tons of use and brought down, quite literally, tons of game. The third is a Pearson Mercury Marauder, the bow I carried for almost a decade from Alaska to Mexico, Africa to South America, and all across the United States. I built it myself at the Pearson plant in Pine Bluff, Arkansas, selecting the wood for the riser from countless billets of Rosewood, tillering the limbs to my own heavy-handed finger pressure and laboring mightily to set the handle to exact specifications. It was a bow I lived with in hundreds of camps, stalked with through countless western aspen patches and trusted beyond a shadow of a doubt. On two occasions, it very probably saved my life (or at least serious abuse), and it put down more really-big animals than any other bow I am ever likely to own.

Today they all stand in a corner of my den, mixed with several other bows of significant, if not as honored, pasts. None of them feel the same as they once did. None of them are ever likely to go hunting with me again; the passage of time affects our muscle, and the evolution of newer (not necessarily better) bow designs erases the aggravation of abused, withering sinew. Doing it really well with something different, and facing the inevitable fact that time has changed my abilities and perhaps my tenacity, seems more important than fighting it.

Occasionally, during moments of contemplation when I'm sitting in my den, I'll pick up the Marauder. There will be a thin coat of dust that I'll remove with an oiled cloth, and something will compel me to brace it. Each time I accomplish the old, push-pull method of stringing it, it requires greater effort.

The carefully fashioned grip no longer feels intimately familiar; in fact, it's almost foreign. There are pictures on the wall with the bow, me and some unlucky beast in a special moment and place that takes me back to those hunts, almost like being there again. In my mind, the four-color scene rolls in, the shot setup is building in instant replay: the bow swings up, fingers tighten on the string, the draw begins and the arrow flies.

Today I have a special bow, a rather battered up Hoyt compound that feels just as good now as the old Marauder once did. It still works pretty well, and I have all the confidence in the world in it, as I did for the old Browning and the one great dog.

I intend to keep my wife for as long as God lets me, though I sincerely suspect I will have no more children; increasing the tribe through the efforts of my children is enough. My shotguns, save one, will be handed across to children, and down to grandchildren, except for the Browning, though, in time, it too will move on.

I expect I will have quite a few more new bows. I give a lot of my old ones away, not too easy, really, being left handed. I might even give the battered Hoyt to someone sometime, but with each passing season that's becoming less likely; we've become quite compatible. Of course, I will keep the three old recurves, there's a lot to be said for playing memory games with old friends even if they are really just sort of ancient tools.

It's not too long now until another hunting season will be here, which brings up another blessing, one that we can all agree on. Although, again, the order of your priorities may vary. I'll stick to mine; you can't enjoy the last one unless you have the others. ▲

Cherished
Subjects

I ssue dates of "vertical" magazines—that's what magazines such as *Petersen's Bowhunting* are called in publishing circles—drive me nuts. Here it is, the beginning of February. The March issue is already out, the next one will be designated May or June or some such warm-weather month, and outside in the backyard my friendly fox squirrel is trying to chip ice off the feeder. It can be confusing, but I don't care.

You see, regardless of what month this issue is published in, I'm quite certain that what is on my mind will be a universally appropriate train of thought when it appears.

Lately, in between the cold arctic blasts that have been crashing down on us, there have been increasing periods of lovely, nearly springlike weather. The days are getting longer. The willow tree outside my window has taken on that interesting shade of golden tan that will soon transform into lime green. My tulip tree has a million buds, some displaying a tinge of faint purple—it's like a few are taking a little peek, looking around very carefully before doing something silly. I have noticed the birds feeding heavily on the rapidly swelling buds.

The squirrel has been cutting the elm tips pretty hard, which I don't understand. I tried one, and it was terrible. Soon she will ignore the sweet offerings in the feeder almost entirely. She has also started her seasonal gnawings on the set of whitetail antlers on the patio—calcium for the kits she's obviously carrying.

In the mornings, which are still quite chilly, the dominant robin has been sitting high up in the mulberry to catch the sun's first warmth. His color has changed lately: He's brighter, shinier than he was in December, and the white ring around his quick eyes almost glows. He sings lustily after the sun warms him up. This week, the old male cardinal that sleeps next door joined him. My wife observed, "Spring's coming. The starlings are starting to build nests on the patio, and they have knocked off some of the covers on the martin's house." I told her the damn things are always building nests and went to find my pellet gun.

If you're like me, once the buds start to show a hint of color here and there, the birds start to sing and big strings of snow geese fly so high you can barely see them heading north, you know it's almost time.

I have always figured that God had a plan to reward serious fishermen and hunters for their winter doldrums and cabin fever. While cable TV and VCRs may help some through those trying times, for many of us, such substitutes are painfully shallow. Obviously, doing away with winter goes strongly against the master plan: folks just have to put up with it, the planet needs it even if we don't and, of course, the entire system started long before TV did. So, there will always be winter, sometimes unbearably long or cold, and sometimes not quite as bad, but it will always be there. Live with it. If you do, at the end will be a reward. You can call your reward what you like, but what I think the Almighty had in mind was crappies and turkeys.

Springtime crappies and turkeys are two of my most cherished subjects. Frankly, I easily place them ahead of whitetail deer! (Oh sacrilege!) While that may be due to the fact that I take a lot more large turkeys than I do large whitetail deer, I don't believe that's the reason. I have given up trying to explain it to friends; it's simply something I have to do.

In the spring, when male turkeys generate a glistening new look and loosen their tonsils with rattling bursts of song, the shallow waters at the north ends of creeks, ponds and lakes warm up, triggering a crappie migration. These two events occur at almost exactly the same time. It is the ultimate reward for the penance of winter.

I hunt turkeys where there is an abundance of water. When I hunt them, I bring a fly/spin combination pack rod, a reel for each and a handful of proper flies and jigs—all tucked neatly in my turkey vest. I carry a small plastic bag for turkey innards suitable for giblets, and a larger one for as many crappies as luck or the law allows. There are some days when both get filled.

It's a lot easier to catch crappies than it is to bow-shoot a turkey. A careful inspection of turkey anatomy quickly reveals a woeful lack of vital target area surrounded by a great deal of nothing vital. Pin-point accuracy—far tighter than when shooting a whitetail—is required.

Lately, some bowhunting turkey gurus of my acquaintance have settled hard on the selection of head shots only. I think that makes a great deal of sense, though there are various opinions on the type of heads used, some suggesting blunts, for instance. Of course, with a shotgun we go for the head, and there are opinions on the proper shot size. Personally, I figure it makes no difference as long as I use sixes! On arrows, I would have to go with broadheads—big broadheads—and of course, blunts aren't legal in many places. I tried the head thing last season and missed both times; it seems more like a task suited for guys that shoot like Chuck Adams or Dwight Schuh. I've always been pretty good, but I have never been really good. Like anything else, you have to make up your own mind—but shoot cleanly, one way or the other.

We are supposed to have a week of nice weather coming up. I'm sure there will be some more cold blasts, too; winter's not over yet. The weather will fight with itself just long enough to mess with our heads. Of course, there will still be some nasty weather when the spring season gets here—wind and rain, that sort of thing. I can kill some turkeys on nasty days once in a while, and I can usually catch crappies on nasty days. And no matter when this issue hits the streets, somewhere a turkey is gobbling or a crappie is biting. By then, maybe I will have tried another head shot. If it doesn't work, I'll spend the rest of the day trying to fill that sack. After all, I catch all my crappies pretty close to their heads. ▲

Big
Game
Downtime

For me, May through June and into July is sort of downtime. There's not a lot going on, and the previous few months were frenzied, so some no-pressure downtime feels good.

To start with, I traveled quite a bit, "on tour" if you will, bopping around the country, making "appearances" at some of the larger deer/turkey shows. They're called "expos" or "classics" more often than "deer shows", and they are pretty neat events. It's fun to watch people at the shows. I get a kick out of all the guys fondling the new hunting gadgets while the wives look on with those pained "you don't need any more stuff" expressions. Admittedly, a lot of gals are really into all the hunting stuff, which I really think is great, but let's face it: Hunting shows are mostly a "toys for boys" kind of thing.

The highlight of these shows is the almost continuous procession of unreal giant bucks carted in for measuring and display. When you go to shows in states like Ohio, Illinois or Wisconsin, big bucks are what you get. Really big bucks. I was told at the Ohio show that there were about 400 deer that scored over 145. As I recall, in Wisconsin there was a six pointer that taped in the 160s. Now, just think about that for a second!

The shows can be long, hard-on-your-feet sort of things, but they're really fun. Of course, you hear a lot of interesting questions. One fellow asked me if Chuck Adams ever missed anything. I told him sure; I was with him in British Columbia once when he missed dinner. Mostly, though, the folks that know me asked if I'd finally caught up with the Big One last season. I just smiled sadly and explained that I'd rather not talk about it. This frequently provokes an attitude of sympathy, which oftentimes leads to hot tips on places I ought to check out. I take notes and maintain a large file for future reference!

So, I toured and appeared. This was just before the turkey season, which I always await anxiously. Around the middle of March, when things start to show a tinge of green, my aging blood begins to percolate. As you might suspect, the shows were loaded with folks selling turkey calls. Apparently the proper way to sell a turkey call is to sit in a booth all day and make turkey noises. This is necessary to convince prospective purchasers that the "Running Redneck Double Beard Long Spur Turkey Tamer Elite Box Call" (constructed from a secret cache of 200-year-old cedar) will out-call any other call in the building.

Now, I do love to call turkeys, but by the time the shows wound down I was largely intolerant of turkey call "experts". Right in the middle of the circuit I took a break and jumped on a plane to celebrate the longbeard opener in the piney-woods plantations of Alabama with my buddy of equal addiction, Trebark guru Jim Crumley. It was a fine celebration, and Crumley's sweet yelps in the open air put things into a proper, more pleasant perspective after that dreadful cacophony of chirping commercialism. With a pair of longbeards over our shoulders, we were at peace—as were, I should point out, the shimmering bronze gobblers we carried with such pride.

The show circuit and other commitments interfered with

my normal foray into Texas to celebrate that opener and, blow of all painful blows, I missed the opener at home in Oklahoma, too. I had specific plans for a bird the size of an emu, a monster I had met in late February. My brother-in-law slew him while I was sitting in a Pope & Young Club board meeting in Michigan. I manfully suggested he deserved it (which he did) and vowed to catch up.

The grind of turkey season—if you're so addicted you just have to be standing in the woods in the predawn of every available morning, rain or shine, tornado alert or no—is especially grueling when you are behind. In my circles, and probably in yours, there is a certain degree of competitiveness relating to the collection of turkeys, or more specifically, turkey spurs. On returning home I was taunted by a pair sufficient in size to rival the claws of a Bengal tiger. Dear brother-in-law's flung gauntlet, on the heels of a historically dull turkey harvesting record, galled me. I hate to be behind!

Daily predawn assaults demand retiring before the chickens, and 100-plus-mile red-eyed round trips before heading to the office are routine, while conversations around the house are short and limited to a single subject. My wife claims Dolly Parton in a bikini would scarcely draw a glance should she prance through the living room when I am in my "spring state". I wonder about that, and conclude she might be right!

It's over now for a while, the touring, and the scrambling after gobblers through the woods in the dark, hoping I wouldn't trip over an old fence or swallow a spider. I've got a new bow to tune up for a summer antelope romp, and Sue's talking about how we should be working over some bluegills. I've just remembered something important: She sometimes wears a bikini when she fishes.

Campfire
Memories

I don't know what it is about campfires, but it seems I am seldom around one when the smoke doesn't find me. Invariably, about the time I'm nice and cozy, it seeks me out and forces me to relocate. It was no different this evening. After hesitating a moment just to be sure it was still after me, I rose, sneezed and went looking for more coffee.

In spite of the fact that they all seem intent on pestering my sinuses and blinding me, I truly do love campfires. Thinking about it, I suspect I have sat in the comforting, warm light of a thousand or more. There have been remote, high-country campfires, usually those quite small, dug deep in soft, loamy duff beneath a copse of some weather-beaten pines that grew crooked from a century of hanging tough against prevailing winds.

They were comforting though, those little fires in their holes with the tiny pack grill laid across. A tin cup that would sear your lips if you weren't careful would eventually heat the precious water for hot chocolate or soup. It was nice to have the soft, golden light of the fire in a place where it was high, wild and lonely.

There have been much larger fires, too, mostly on the flat, lonesome deserts of Arizona, Nevada and California—almost conflagrations really of stacked greasewood or mesquite started "White-Man" style with a splash of gas. We did that when we were desert rats, when varmint calling was our passion and the nights were as cold as the stars that watched. They were fun fires filled with the boisterous companionship of a dozen or so guys who would scatter far and wide in two-man teams when it was time to see if the coyotes and cats wanted to come. I suppose, before they burned down low enough for the steaks and beans, our fires could have been seen for 50 miles.

There is something about African campfires like few others I've experienced. Sure, maybe just because it's Africa where almost every evening there was something new and exciting to celebrate. You could sit there until very late and talk about it. Like the sable, and how lucky you were that there was just enough room where he stopped to slip an arrow through. You could talk about it until a deep-purple night finished a day you would never have again. And when it was time to go to bed, the fire was tired, too.

There have been fires in other places far, far from home, like the ones on a small island on a big lake as far north as you can get in Alberta, Canada, which have given me serious cause to reflect on our planet, the universe and God. It was to be an adventure with packs and canoes; an expedition, more than just a bowhunt for moose and bear.

That fire burned constantly. Light rain transformed to sleet, sleet to heavy wet flakes. The snow came and stayed; the wind howled, laid, caught its breath and came back. The fire was our companion under the lean-to. We stood by it, sat by it, lived by it. The days were long, dull and colorless, but the nights could sometimes be awesome. The northern lights, aurora borealis, reflections of sun and ice bounced back and forth from earth to sky, flickered and danced through broken waves of scudding clouds. Those were nights to make you wonder, to talk quietly of many things. They were nights when you realized how very big most things are, and what an insignificant role you play in the scheme of things. The fire burned until the plane could finally come. We left having never seen a moose or a bear. I didn't really care.

Some fires are impromptu, necessary little things, like on the afternoon some years ago when I shot a bull elk in Colorado. It was drizzling steadily when we came together. I had still-hunted behind the fresh tracks of the traveling band for an hour or so when the mews and chirps of cows and calves signaled I was catching up. From hands and knees I could see their legs in the thick, dark timber. I was crawling ever so carefully forward when the bull stood up 20 yards to my right. Sometimes you are lucky and they hold when they should not. He stood still too long. Field-dressing a wet, slippery elk is not easy all alone. By the time I had him support tied and emptied, the sweat from my exertion mingling with the chilling drizzle clutched me in a trembling grip. Beneath the canopy of an ancient spruce I fumbled to start a small fire. With my back to the gnarled spruce, the heat reflecting from the compact aluminum space blanket eased my shivering chill. I was soon warmed—and hungry.

I do not believe there are any better campfires than the ones you share with your kids. The first ones as they grow up, where they start to learn a bit about what life, bowhunting and the outdoors is all about. Of course, with those first ones you had to have hot dogs and marshmallows in camp. A campfire without marshmallows would never do. The campfires get better as the children grow, gain experience, confidence and achieve increasing levels of success. Maybe they seem better because they learned to gather wood, set up camp and start the fire themselves, becoming full partners. Then they grow and scatter to their own campfires, some nearly as far from home as you have been and you are not all together as often. It's the way of things: Neither good times nor bad last forever.

At the edge of the fire, away from the smoke, I found the coffeepot cooling. Refilled, still hot enough, I wandered to the edge of camp where the soft light played on the white belly hair of my partner's buck hanging in the shadows. Nice eight pointer, good spread, typically thin-horned for this part of the country. I rattled him up on the third set of the afternoon after a cool front had passed through and the wind laid. I never saw the buck. I heard him coming, stop, the soft thump of the bow, followed by an audible "thwock". When I looked my amigo was standing with a look on his face he probably hasn't had since he got his first serious kiss. Same difference, this was a first time, too.

I went back to the fire to sit and finish the coffee. It is almost all coals flaring now. The breeze flirts with it pushing up weak fingers of smoke. I'll sit here 'til the smoke finds me again.

Just Looking Things Over

I went out the other day just poking around. Took my bow and varmint call, loaded the bow quiver with a combination of broadheads and Judos. Thought I might shoot at a squirrel, maybe call up a coyote, plink at some cow pies, shadows and clumps of grass. There hasn't been much going on lately. The weather has been typical Oklahoma: zipping back and forth, up and down, too dry, too wet.

Yesterday the wind blew every direction but straight up. Too much rain has screwed up the fishing; the ponds look like chocolate malts, but I figured the wind had dried out the rutted ranch roads enough so I wouldn't be skidding sideways much, except for in the long, greasy flat spot across the top of Bull Meadows. I've been stuck on the ranch three times in 10 years, twice in the greasy slop at the top of Bull Meadows.

I thought I'd wander a bit. I needed to check on a couple of my tree stands to see if the squirrels had eaten the foam rubber off the seats. I probably should have taken them down at the end of the season, but I didn't. Lazy, I suppose, or getting old. Both, I reckon! I have a tripod stand in a clump of skimpy post oak. I needed to see if the wasps or hornets—I'm not sure exactly which except they're mean buggers—were setting up housekeeping in the hollow metal legs. I climbed up it one day a couple years ago before the season opened and disturbed a whole flock of them. Not too good of an experience.

Now, I remember to approach the tripod carefully armed with a can of hornet spray. Boy, does that knock their socks off. Kind of like skeet shooting with a hose! I made sure a can was in the truck box along with a can of Permanone for the ticks and chiggers. I've never understood a need for ticks and chiggers. I'm pretty nervous about ticks. A new strain of spotted fever just about carried my wife off a few years ago. Scary, and now we have Lyme's to worry about, too, along with recluse spiders, copperheads and buzztails. Makes you wonder if you shouldn't just stay inside. Not hardly!

I went to the tripod first. Shot several dried-up flops on the way in, missed a couple others. Shooting pretty good, though. The tripod is in a killer location, a little point of timber at the head of a subtle draw that comes out of a pretty rugged canyon. I shot a good buck there last season, a real high-racked eight pointer with solid mass though he didn't have much spread and his third points were a bit short. So what! He's a fine buck.

No squadron of irate bugs were living in the hollow legs. I was happy about that. Slipped the spray can back in my daypack and wandered off to the east where the timber ends and the bluestem prairie takes off for somewhere a long ways away, a good place to call up a coyote. We have lots of coyotes, too many I'm thinking—they raise serious hell with the fawn crop. The bobcats do, too.

I found a spot in some good-sized rocks to call from where my outline was broken up, and I could lay my loaded Hoyt Striker on a benchlike boulder close at hand. It's pretty easy to call by yourself when you have a rifle or shotgun, something I do quite often when I'm real, real serious. It's tougher with a bow, of course, too much commotion getting it up and drawn. Fun to try, though.

I hadn't called a minute when a bobcat about the size of a Bengal tiger trotted in bold as you please and sat down 15 yards away just looking. Bobcat season ended February 28! The State of Oklahoma, that is to say the Department of Wildlife Conservation, extended the bobcat season a month longer this year because, in simple terms, we have too many bobcats. They also increased the season limit from eight to 20.

I came up here three times in January and February to call and shoot some bobcats. Never called one up at the first stand, which dented my ego pretty good because allegedly I am a bona-fide critter-calling expert. Now, I'm confronted with one of the biggest, prettiest, well-spotted male cats I've ever seen in Oklahoma, and he's just as safe as if he was in God's pocket.

I stood bow in hand, tempted. He looked me over indifferently, his large yellow eyes with inky black pupils widening slightly, then he turned and walked off flicking his white-tipped tail every other step.

I wandered again, heading north toward the fence line that separates Kansas from Oklahoma, then west down into the canyon where, if I was calling bobcats, is exactly where I would choose to do it. Not at the edge of the prairie where I just did. I found a pretty good shed, five pointer, doubled with 16 inches inside, maybe 135. I wonder where he was when I was looking for him last November. It's nice to know he's still around.

I made one more call from the cover of a little cedar as the afternoon shadows began to stretch toward the east. Nothing showed except two crows that coasted in screeching furiously.

Altogether, I guess I meandered over a five-mile circle. I found another shed, a forked horn. Estimated total score:

about 40. There was the dried-out hull of what once was a deer hanging caught by the back legs on the borderline fence. Coyotes had carried off the front half so I don't know if it was a buck or a doe. I had met a bobcat I hope to meet again—and I figure the owner of the shed still lives near the canyon—and this season he should be bigger. I shot quite a few arrows, most pretty well. It felt good just wandering, plinking arrows and looking things over.

Just poking around. Not a bad way to spend a day. ▲

Sage
Advice

It was put to me suddenly and knocked the socks off my plans when my doctors told me I would lose the tail end of my hunting season last year. Recovery time from the surgeries—there would be at least three—was unknown, but it was safe to assume it would extend well beyond the remaining month of the Oklahoma season and cut into a couple of January and February excursions I was really looking forward to as well.

This hunting news generated a sense of urgency—panic, actually—far greater than any apprehensions of being carved upon. December's when I go into serious freezer mode. The contents of my freezer were embarrassingly skimpy, and the projected time frame gave me less than a week to fix the problem. Further, scalpels in the hands of skilled surgeons are much easier to face than a wife's cocked eyebrow when, after rummaging through said freezer, she can find nothing to cook that stirs her culinary spirit, a condition provoking incriminations toward husbands who spend countless hours afield seeking antlers—"that you cannot eat!"—while letting juicy does walk, or worse, who shoot a nice juicy deer out of state and give it away. I give up. Guilty as charged!

Tying the elements of surgery, a meagerly stocked freezer and a mildly aggravated wife together might seem a bit of a stretch for Trail's End. Yet, as I pondered, it seemed clear they projected the possibility of offering some sound advice. For openers, let's begin with the surgeries.

It's not that I had them, rather it's what caused them that warrants this discussion in sincere hope it will save others a) serious discomfort, b) loss of valuable bowhunting time or c) their life. Pick one that seems most important, and we'll continue from here.

I haven't a clue as to how many forms of cancer there are or what causes most of them, other than there's way too many. I do know we're told there are things we all can and should do to prevent some types. Sometimes we're told that what science has suggested we should have been doing doesn't really work or, in fact, might actually be a cause. However, in the matter of sun-induced skin cancers—two kinds now—I have some experience and am here to report that the insidious potential of the same can scare you clear into next year.

I grew up in an era when sunscreen was pretty much a nonentity. Instead, we had tanning solutions and baby oil with which to baste ourselves in the need for summertime-bronzed skin; but they offered no protection. I spent uncountable hours fishing big water where reflective sun rays bombarded me from all angles, and I backpacked through miles of alpine high country where clean, clear air increased their penetration. I bowhunted the sunny desert for jackrabbits and called coyotes across snowy landscapes on bright, windless days. Sun and wind burn was a constant condition; and serious damage, though it would lay hidden for many years, had been done.

Today we should be very much aware of how dangerous exposure to the sun's rays can be, and we now have fine sun-screening products in a wide range of gradients to protect us. Yet, in a time when health and healthy ways is so prominently upbeat, I still see the threat of ultraviolet rays being commonly ignored in the hunting and fishing camps that I frequent.

At the onset, these problem seem no more than minor irritations; subtle changes in a mole or skin blemish—itchy, flaky, discolored, different, easy to ignore. The kicker's what appears to be superficial might very well be deep. If something looks or feels different, don't procrastinate. See your doctor. This is good advice and insurance against losing precious hunting time, or something even worse.

Speaking of hunting time, I was rapidly running out when Pete—aka The Judge—called to state he had a new place to look at. I love wandering over new places, and this one seemed made to order for a last-ditch effort. A meandering brush-choked creek bottom loaded with deer sign with evidence a few bucks were still working scrapes bisected a section of rolling bluestem prairie. A beaver dam to the north formed a natural funnel that was pockmarked with tracks. "Oh Boy!" I thought, and I strapped up my Baby Grand.

The late-afternoon sun turned the prairie to a rolling stretch of gold scratched with fingers of blue shadow. I could hear it a long time before I finally made out the flicker of a rear leg through the brush. Then I could see it was a chunky young six-point, though my adrenaline surge was checked by the fact he was on the far side of the beaver pond. "He won't come to me from there," I fretted. But, he did. Amazingly, he jumped into the pond and swam toward my side. All the lights in my system went on green; freezer mode was about to be affected.

Now comes the last of my tidbits of sage advice. Never cut and wrap them before they are tagged and bagged.

In my mind I could smell liver and onions and see Sue smiling in the kitchen as she marinated thick steaks. In real time I watched the chartreuse fletching flash beneath his chest, stood open-mouthed on the stand as his flag-waving bounds faded in the thickening gloom, and uttered a rather strong word.

Oh, one thing more about bowhunting. There's no such thing as a gimme if you don't pick a spot.